BEST OF THE

Pillsbury

Bake-Off®

WILEY

WILEY PUBLISHING, INC.

LIBRARY OF CONGRESS CATALOGING-IN-PUBLICATION DATA

Pillsbury best of the bake-off cookies and bars.
        p., cm.
    Includes index.
    ISBN 978-0-470-11138-3 (pbk.)
    1. Cookies. 2. Bars (Desserts) I. Pillsbury-Washburn Flour Mills Company.
TX772.P486 2008
641.8'654--dc22

                                        2007011316

Manufactured in the United States of America

10 9 8 7 6 5 4 3 2

Cover photo: Caramel-Filled Chocolate Cookies (page 28)

GENERAL MILLS

Publisher, Cookbooks
Maggie Gilbert/Lynn Vettel

Manager, Cookbooks
Lois Tlusty

Editor
Lori Fox

Food Editor
Lola Whalen

Recipe Development and Testing
Pillsbury Kitchens

Photography
General Mills Photography Studios and Image Library

WILEY PUBLISHING, INC.

Publisher
Natalie Chapman

Executive Editor
Anne Ficklen

Senior Editorial Assistant
Charleen Barila

Production Editor
Amy Zarkos

Cover Design
Suzanne Sunwoo

Art Director
Tai Blanche

Photography Art Direction
Chris Everett/Boom Island

Prop Stylist
Michelle Joy

Manufacturing Manager
Kevin Watt

Our recipes have been tested in the Pillsbury Kitchens and meet our standards of easy preparation, reliability and great taste.

For more great recipes, visit pillsbury.com

contents

the Bake-Off® contest through the years

There is nothing like the Pillsbury Bake-Off® Contest.

Have you ever made something so good that you just had to share it? Or tweaked a recipe until it was just right? Or nervously waited as the family took the first bite of a new dish?

Then you've experienced a Bake-Off® Contest.

Like everyday cooks around the country, Pillsbury Bake-Off® winners envisioned making a dish so yummy that family and friends would ask for more.

Of course, the Bake-Off® Contest is a little different. A panel of judges try that first bite. Ninety-nine other cooks share "your" kitchen. But the pay-off for your great recipe is a million times more lucrative than usual.

Whether you're a finalist at a Pillsbury Bake-Off® Contest or simply a star in your own kitchen, you share something special. Both you and Bake-Off® contestants know the food you developed with love for your family will become treasured family recipes in someone's home.

1950s

The first Pillsbury Bake-Off® Contest spurred a phenomenon that many copied but few have perfected over the years. Throughout the '50s, the annual Bake-Off® Contest showcased the creativity of America's best home cooks and their favorite new flavors in the kitchen. The fictitious everywoman Ann Pillsbury—aka The Pillsbury Lady—presided over the contest and its innovative magazines. Ann encouraged cooks young and old to share a "love of good baked things that is so very strong in our country." Reflecting mid-century interest in the glamorous home, the contest was held at New York City's Waldorf-Astoria Hotel, where it resided for many years. The contest showcased kitchen innovations including a white General Electric four-burner, double-oven. By the late '50s, electric mixers, another labor- and time-saving device, were introduced in each cook's "kitchen" at the contest. In the early years, every recipe included Pillsbury BEST® enriched flour.

1960s

In the 1960s, the "Busy Lady" was a Bake-Off® theme. Bake-Off® recipes were "shortcutted, streamlined and up-to-dated for you" by Pillsbury. Although the heart of the home was still the kitchen in the 1960s, the fact that many women led busy lives outside of the kitchen meant everyday cooks created easy but delicious meals for their families. While it "used to take all day to make a bread," the prizewinning Chicken Little Bread promised a great homemade loaf in less time. In 1967, the official Bake-Off® magazine featured shortcuts to prize recipes and offered "homemade goodness with hurry-up timing" to the average family cook. At the Bake-Off® Contest, the self-cleaning oven made its debut, and fresh refrigerated biscuit and crescent roll doughs were used as key ingredients for the first time. In 1969, the contest changed forever when it introduced "three divisions"—flour, mix and fresh refrigerated dough—each with a $10,000 Grand Prize. The best recipe won a $25,000 cash prize.

1970s

By 1972, Ann Pillsbury had disappeared from the Bake-Off® Contest, but a new icon had taken her place. The Pillsbury Doughboy, in a cowboy hat, graced the cover of the 1972 Bake-Off® recipe collection. His friendly face would remain a standing symbol of the contest for some time to come. The Doughboy's cowboy hat symbolized more than a friendly demeanor. It signaled the Bake-Off® Contest was on the move. Houston, New Orleans, San Diego and San Francisco were new sites for the contest and reflected America's growing diversity and shifts in population away from the East Coast. Celebrity hosts and judges awarded prizes on Bake-Off® day. By the early 1970s, the "health" food craze was recognizable in the Bake-Off® Contest. Many recipes featured apples, carrots, whole wheat, oats and granola, but most contestant recipes reflected a lack of time for cooking. In the mid-1970s, the Bake-Off® recipe collection cost around a dollar and included recipes developed for the newest kitchen innovation, the microwave oven.

1980s

In the mid-1980s, the Bake-Off® Contest offered a fast-forward cuisine of quick and easy recipes, snacks and a new entrant to the arena, ethnic recipes. Competitors brought a wide variety of ethnic backgrounds to the contest. Wontons and Mexican-style recipes popped on the Bake-Off® scene for the first time. The microwave acquired a place in almost every home in the '80s, and many finalists used a microwave to prepare part or all of their entries in a matter of minutes. A microwave category was a new category at the contest. High-spending style was a hallmark of the '80s, and the Bake-Off® Contest followed suit. The Grand Prize increased to $40,000, and first-place winners in each of five categories won $15,000 for their favorite family recipes. Celebrities continued to be featured hosts, and in 1983, Bob Barker, longtime host of the TV show *The Price Is Right*, awarded more than $130,000 in cash prizes in San Diego.

1990s

Although the theme "quick and easy" had been a staple at past Bake-Off® Contests, for the first time in 1998, Quick & Easy was its own category in the contest, increasing the number of Bake-Off® categories to five. The categories—30-Minute Main Dishes, Simple Side Dishes, Fast and Easy Treats, and Quick Snacks and Appetizers—all reflected the changing nature of the American kitchen. What changed in the kitchen? Time, more than ever, was in short supply for families with jobs, hobbies and kids, but a desire to give families the best food that mom—or dad—could make was never compromised by Bake-Off® contestants. The contest entered the modern era on February 26, 1996, when more than $1,054,000 in cash and prizes were awarded for the first time. The first million-dollar winner was Macadamia Fudge Torte, a recipe developed by Kurt Wait of California, one of 14 men whose recipes were chosen for the contest.

2000s

At the turn of the century, the Bake-Off® Contest turned 50! After all these years, the contest is still about creating great food while reflecting the changing nature of American society. In the first decade of the new century, the Bake-Off® Contest offered adventurous flavors that blurred ethnic boundaries. For the first time, recipes could be entered in the contest in Spanish. Bolder, even exotic, flavors came to the forefront as American cooks encountered a variety of cooking styles both at home and in travels around the world. In the 2000s, the number of Bake-Off® categories increased to six. Dinner Made Easy, Wake Up to Breakfast, Simple Snacks, Weekends Made Special, the empty-nest direction of Cooking for Two and a healthy cooking category, Brand New You, reflected a trend set by health-conscious American cooks.

cookies and bars through the decades

Recipes are a reflection of our changing tastes and of our changing times as well. The Pillsbury Bake-Off® Contest entries mark a moment in history that reflects "what's for dessert" and what's happening in American homes.

1950s

In early Bake-Off® contests, the one required ingredient for entry was Pillsbury BEST® Flour, so it's not surprising that baked goods represented the largest category of entries during the contest's first decade. Most women worked in the home and spent a great deal of time in the kitchen. Homemakers didn't have the kind of access to supermarkets we enjoy today, so most of these early cookie and bar recipes called for ordinary pantry ingredients and were destined as an after-school snack or to be taken to a party or a school event.

Popular '50s Bake-Off® cookie and bar recipes:
- Starlight Mint Surprise Cookies
- Snappy Turtle Cookies
- Ginger Cookie Capers

1960s

During the '60s, women led busy lives at home, in their communities and in leisure activities. Women had less time to spare in the kitchen and eagerly turned to convenience foods and time-saving appliances for help. In 1966, the Bake-Off® contest's "Busy Lady" theme recognized the growing trend of convenience cooking with simplified recipes. Two products in particular—refrigerated dough and cake mix—were new at the time and both played a role in the Bake-Off® dessert entries during this decade.

Popular '60s Bake-Off® cookie and bar recipes:
- Oatmeal Carmelitas
- Fudge-Nut Layer Bars
- Candy Bar Cookies

1970s

"Natural" ingredients were buzzwords during the Bake-Off® contests of the '70s. Homey baked goods featured ingredients like molasses, bananas and oats. There wasn't much happening in the way of cake and pie innovation—in fact, pie baking as a whole was on the decline—but pie-like bar cookies, or "squares," were becoming increasingly common.

Popular '70s Bake-Off® cookie and bar recipes:
- Pecan Pie Surprise Bars
- Chocolate-Cherry Bars
- Crispy Date Bars

Treasure Chest Bars (page 86)

1980s

The '80s were the decade of decadence, and the Bake-Off® dessert entries from that time mimic this trend. Fancy, indulgent cookies and bars were popular, and cooks turned to Europe for inspiration. Time continued to be a precious commodity and consumers made desserts for entertaining rather than everyday meals. Four of the five Grand Prize–winning recipes of this decade were cakes or tarts.

Popular '80s Bake-Off® cookie and bar recipes:

- Salted Peanut Chews
- White Chocolate Chunk Cookies
- Peanut Butter 'n Fudge Brownies

1990s

In the '90s, recipes reflected our global community with the most diverse ethnic cuisines ever. Gourmet ingredients became more mainstream, and cooks displayed increased sophistication by combining the best of European and American traditions. Recipes were inspired by the explosion in availability and variety of products, such as candy bars and toppings.

Popular '90s Bake-Off® cookie and bar recipes:

- Fudgy Bonbons
- Black and White Brownies
- Caramel-Pecan Sticky Bun Cookies

2000s

At the turn of the century, technology influenced consumer tastes, and desserts were no exception. For the first time, more than three-quarters of all Bake-Off® recipes were submitted online. Savvy and sophisticated trendsetters reflected major changes in food and culture as Americans enjoyed easy access to the Internet and cable television. Despite these trends, cookies and bars remained a reminder of the simple life at home.

Popular 2000s Bake-Off® cookie and bar recipes:

- Chewy Chocolate–Peanut Butter Bars
- Cinnamon-Toffee-Pecan Cookies
- Almond-Toffee-Mocha Squares

Rocky Road Fudge Bars (page 21) ▶

most requested cookies & bars

chocolate chip–peanut butter squares

BARRY GARCIA

West Palm Beach, FL

Bake-Off® Contest 38, 1998

12 BARS

PREP TIME: *15 minutes*

START TO FINISH: *2 hours 20 minutes*

1½ cups powdered sugar

1½ cups creamy peanut butter

1½ teaspoons vanilla

1 roll (16.5 oz) Pillsbury® Create 'n Bake™ refrigerated chocolate chip cookies

1 Heat oven to 350°F. In medium bowl, mix powdered sugar, peanut butter and vanilla with spoon until well blended.

2 Cut cookie dough in half crosswise. In ungreased 8- or 9-inch square pan, break up half of the dough. With floured fingers, press dough evenly in bottom of pan.

3 Press peanut butter mixture evenly over dough. Crumble and sprinkle remaining half of dough over peanut butter mixture. Carefully spread as evenly as possible.

4 Bake 30 to 35 minutes or until golden brown and firm to the touch. Cool in pan on cooling rack 30 minutes. Refrigerate until chilled, about 1 hour. For bars, cut into 4 rows by 3 rows. Serve chilled or at room temperature.

High Altitude (3500–6500 ft): Bake 33 to 38 minutes.

1 Bar: Calories 430 (Calories from Fat 210); Total Fat 23g (Saturated Fat 5g; Trans Fat 1.5g); Cholesterol 5mg; Sodium 270mg; Total Carbohydrate 45g (Dietary Fiber 2g; Sugars 32g); Protein 9g **% Daily Value:** Vitamin A 0%; Vitamin C 0%; Calcium 0%; Iron 6% **Exchanges:** ½ Starch, 2½ Other Carbohydrate, 1 High-Fat Meat, 3 Fat **Carbohydrate Choices:** 3

apple crisp crescent bars

PEGGY VANPATTEN

Antioch, IL

Bake-Off® Contest 24, 1973

36 BARS

PREP TIME: *20 minutes*

START TO FINISH: *1 hour 50 minutes*

BARS

4 cups thinly sliced peeled apples (4 medium)

¼ cup granulated sugar

1 tablespoon Pillsbury BEST® all-purpose flour

1 teaspoon ground cinnamon

1 can (8 oz) Pillsbury® refrigerated crescent dinner rolls

TOPPING

1 cup packed brown sugar

¾ cup quick-cooking or old-fashioned oats

½ cup Pillsbury BEST® all-purpose flour

¼ cup butter or margarine, softened

2 teaspoons vanilla

1 Heat oven to 375°F. In large bowl, mix apples, granulated sugar, 1 tablespoon flour and the cinnamon.

2 Unroll dough into 2 long rectangles. Place rectangles in ungreased 15 × 10 × 1-inch pan; gently press dough to cover bottom of pan, sealing perforations. Spoon apple mixture over dough.

3 In medium bowl, mix all topping ingredients until crumbly; sprinkle over apple mixture.

4 Bake 22 to 27 minutes or until golden brown and apples are tender. Cool completely in pan on cooling rack, about 1 hour. For bars, cut into 6 rows by 6 rows.

High Altitude (3500–6500 ft): Bake 27 to 32 minutes.

1 Bar: Calories 90 (Calories from Fat 25); Total Fat 3g (Saturated Fat 1.5g; Trans Fat 0g); Cholesterol 0mg; Sodium 60mg; Total Carbohydrate 14g (Dietary Fiber 0g; Sugars 9g); Protein 0g **% Daily Value:** Vitamin A 0%; Vitamin C 0%; Calcium 0%; Iron 2% **Exchanges:** 1 Other Carbohydrate, ½ Fat **Carbohydrate Choices:** 1

chocolate-cherry bars

48 BARS

PREP TIME: *15 minutes*

START TO FINISH: *2 hours*

FRANCIS I. JERZAK
Porter, MN
Bake-Off® Contest 25, 1974

1 Heat oven to 350°F (325°F for dark or nonstick pan). Grease 15 × 10 × 1-inch or 13 × 9-inch pan with shortening or cooking spray; lightly flour. In large bowl, mix all bar ingredients with spoon until well blended. Spread in pan.

2 Bake until toothpick inserted in center comes out clean. Bake 15 × 10 × 1-inch pan 20 to 30 minutes; bake 13 × 9-inch pan 25 to 30 minutes.

3 In small saucepan, mix sugar, milk and butter. Heat to boiling. Boil 1 minute, stirring constantly. Remove from heat. Stir in chocolate chips until smooth. Pour and spread over warm bars. Cool completely in pan on cooling rack, about 1 hour 15 minutes. For bars, cut into 8 rows by 6 rows.

High Altitude (3500–6500 ft): Heat oven to 350°F (325°F for dark or nonstick pan). Bake 15 × 10 × 1-inch pan 25 to 35 minutes; bake 13 × 9-inch pan 30 to 35 minutes.

BARS

1 box (18.25 oz) Pillsbury® Moist Supreme® devil's food cake mix

1 can (21 oz) cherry pie filling

1 teaspoon almond extract

2 eggs, beaten

FROSTING

1 cup sugar

⅓ cup milk

5 tablespoons butter or margarine

1 cup semisweet chocolate chips (6 oz)

1 Bar: Calories 110 (Calories from Fat 30); Total Fat 3.5g (Saturated Fat 2g; Trans Fat 0g); Cholesterol 10mg; Sodium 95mg; Total Carbohydrate 19g (Dietary Fiber 0g; Sugars 14g); Protein 1g **% Daily Value:** Vitamin A 0%; Vitamin C 0%; Calcium 0%; Iron 2% **Exchanges:** 1½ Other Carbohydrate, ½ Fat **Carbohydrate Choices:** 1

salted peanut chews

GERTRUDE M. SCHWEITZERHOF
Cupertino, CA
Bake-Off® Contest 29, 1980

36 BARS

PREP TIME: *35 minutes*
START TO FINISH: *1 hour 35 minutes*

BASE

1½ cups Pillsbury BEST®
   all-purpose flour

⅔ cup packed brown sugar

½ teaspoon baking powder

½ teaspoon salt

¼ teaspoon baking soda

½ cup butter or margarine, softened

1 teaspoon vanilla

2 egg yolks

3 cups miniature marshmallows

TOPPING

⅔ cup corn syrup

¼ cup butter or margarine

2 teaspoons vanilla

1 bag (10 oz) peanut butter chips
   (1⅔ cups)

2 cups crisp rice cereal

2 cups salted peanuts

1 Heat oven to 350°F. In large bowl, beat all base ingredients except marshmallows with electric mixer on low speed until crumbly. Press mixture firmly in bottom of ungreased 13 × 9-inch pan.

2 Bake 12 to 15 minutes or until light golden brown. Immediately sprinkle marshmallows evenly over base; bake 1 to 2 minutes longer or until marshmallows just begin to puff. Cool while preparing topping.

3 In 3-quart saucepan, mix all topping ingredients except cereal and peanuts. Heat over low heat, stirring constantly, just until chips are melted and mixture is smooth. Remove from heat. Stir in cereal and peanuts. Immediately spoon warm topping over marshmallows; spread to cover. Refrigerate until firm, about 45 minutes. For bars, cut into 6 rows by 6 rows.

High Altitude (3500–6500 ft): Heat oven to 375°F.

1 Bar: Calories 200 (Calories from Fat 100); Total Fat 11g (Saturated Fat 3.5g; Trans Fat 0g); Cholesterol 20mg; Sodium 130mg; Total Carbohydrate 22g (Dietary Fiber 1g; Sugars 13g); Protein 4g **% Daily Value:** Vitamin A 2%; Vitamin C 0%; Calcium 0%; Iron 4% **Exchanges:** 1½ Other Carbohydrate, ½ High-Fat Meat, 1½ Fat **Carbohydrate Choices:** 1½

Pillsbury Best of the Bake-Off® Cookies & Bars

pecan pie surprise bars

MRS. PEARL HALL
Snohomish, WA
Bake-Off® Contest 22, 1971

36 BARS

PREP TIME: *15 minutes*
START TO FINISH: *1 hour 55 minutes*

BASE

1 box (18.25 oz) Pillsbury® Moist
   Supreme® classic yellow cake mix

⅓ cup butter or margarine, softened

1 egg

FILLING

Reserved ⅔ cup dry cake mix

½ cup packed brown sugar

1½ cups dark corn syrup

1 teaspoon vanilla

3 eggs

1 cup chopped pecans

1 Heat oven to 350°F. Grease 13 × 9-inch pan with shortening or cooking spray. Reserve ⅔ cup of the dry cake mix for filling. In large bowl, beat remaining dry cake mix, the butter and 1 egg with electric mixer on low speed until well blended. Press in bottom of pan.

2 Bake 15 to 20 minutes or until light golden brown. Meanwhile, in large bowl, beat reserved ⅔ cup dry cake mix, the brown sugar, corn syrup, vanilla and 3 eggs on low speed until moistened. Beat on medium speed 1 minute or until well blended.

3 Pour filling mixture over warm base; sprinkle with pecans.

4 Bake 30 to 35 minutes longer or until filling is set. Cool completely in pan on cooling rack, about 45 minutes. For bars, cut into 6 rows by 6 rows. Store in refrigerator.

High Altitude (3500–6500 ft): Heat oven to 375°F. Stir ⅓ cup all-purpose flour into dry cake mix before removing ⅔ cup for filling. Decrease dark corn syrup to 1¼ cup.

1 Bar: Calories 160 (Calories from Fat 50); Total Fat 6g (Saturated Fat 2g; Trans Fat 0g); Cholesterol 30mg; Sodium 120mg; Total Carbohydrate 26g (Dietary Fiber 0g; Sugars 15g); Protein 1g **% Daily Value:** Vitamin A 0%; Vitamin C 0%; Calcium 2%; Iron 2% **Exchanges:** ½ Starch, 1 Other Carbohydrate, 1 Fat **Carbohydrate Choices:** 2

quick crescent pecan pie bars

24 BARS

PREP TIME: *10 minutes*

START TO FINISH: *1 hour 35 minutes*

ALBINA FLIELLER
Floresville, TX
Bake-Off® Contest 24, 1973

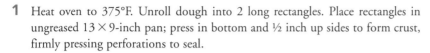

1 Heat oven to 375°F. Unroll dough into 2 long rectangles. Place rectangles in ungreased 13 × 9-inch pan; press in bottom and ½ inch up sides to form crust, firmly pressing perforations to seal.

2 Bake crust 5 minutes. Meanwhile, in medium bowl, mix all filling ingredients.

3 Pour filling over partially baked crust. Bake 18 to 22 minutes longer or until golden brown. Cool completely in pan on cooling rack, about 1 hour. For bars, cut into 6 rows by 4 rows.

High Altitude (3500–6500 ft): In step 2, bake crust 7 minutes.

CRUST

1 can (8 oz) Pillsbury® refrigerated crescent dinner rolls

FILLING

1 egg, beaten

½ cup chopped pecans

½ cup sugar

½ cup corn syrup

1 tablespoon butter or margarine, melted

½ teaspoon vanilla

1 Bar: Calories 100 (Calories from Fat 40); Total Fat 4.5g (Saturated Fat 1g; Trans Fat 0.5g); Cholesterol 10mg; Sodium 85mg; Total Carbohydrate 14g (Dietary Fiber 0g; Sugars 8g); Protein 1g **% Daily Value:** Vitamin A 0%; Vitamin C 0%; Calcium 0%; Iron 0% **Exchanges:** 1 Other Carbohydrate, 1 Fat **Carbohydrate Choices:** 1

oatmeal carmelitas

ERLYCE LARSON
Kennedy, MN
Bake-Off® Contest 18, 1967

36 BARS

PREP TIME: *30 minutes*
START TO FINISH: *2 hours 55 minutes*

BASE

2 cups Pillsbury BEST® all-purpose flour

2 cups quick-cooking oats

1½ cups packed brown sugar

1 teaspoon baking soda

½ teaspoon salt

1¼ cups butter or margarine, softened

FILLING

1 jar (12.5 oz) caramel topping (1 cup)

3 tablespoons Pillsbury BEST®
all-purpose flour

1 cup semisweet chocolate chips (6 oz)

½ cup chopped nuts

1 Heat oven to 350°F. Grease 13 × 9-inch pan with shortening or cooking spray. In large bowl, beat all base ingredients with electric mixer on low speed until crumbly. Reserve half of crumb mixture (about 3 cups) for topping. Press remaining crumb mixture in bottom of pan.

2 Bake 10 minutes. Meanwhile, in small bowl, mix caramel topping and 3 tablespoons flour.

3 Sprinkle chocolate chips and nuts over partially baked base. Drizzle evenly with caramel mixture; sprinkle with reserved crumb mixture.

4 Bake 18 to 22 minutes longer or until golden brown. Cool completely in pan on cooling rack, about 1 hour. Refrigerate until filling is set, 1 to 2 hours. For bars, cut into 6 rows by 6 rows. Store in tightly covered container.

High Altitude (3500–6500 ft): No change.

1 Bar: Calories 200 (Calories from Fat 80); Total Fat 9g (Saturated Fat 5g; Trans Fat 0g); Cholesterol 15mg; Sodium 150mg; Total Carbohydrate 27g (Dietary Fiber 1g; Sugars 16g); Protein 2g **% Daily Value:** Vitamin A 4%; Vitamin C 0%; Calcium 2%; Iron 6% **Exchanges:** ½ Starch, 1½ Other Carbohydrate, 1½ Fat **Carbohydrate Choices:** 2

quick 'n' chewy crescent bars

ISABELLE COLLINS
Ramona, CA
Bake-Off® Contest 23, 1972

48 BARS

PREP TIME: *15 minutes*
START TO FINISH: *1 hour 30 minutes*

1 cup coconut
¾ cup packed brown sugar
½ cup Pillsbury BEST® all-purpose flour
½ cup chopped pecans
¼ cup butter or margarine
1 can (8 oz) Pillsbury® refrigerated crescent dinner rolls
1 can (14 oz) sweetened condensed milk (not evaporated)

1 Heat oven to 400°F. In medium bowl, mix coconut, brown sugar, flour and pecans. With pastry blender or fork, cut in butter until mixture resembles coarse crumbs. Set aside.

2 Unroll dough into 2 long rectangles. Place rectangles in ungreased 15 × 10 × 1-inch pan; press in bottom of pan, firmly pressing perforations to seal.

3 Pour condensed milk evenly over dough; spread to within ½ inch of edges. Sprinkle coconut mixture over condensed milk; press in lightly.

4 Bake 12 to 15 minutes or until deep golden brown. Cool completely in pan on cooling rack, about 1 hour. For bars, cut into 8 rows by 6 rows.

High Altitude (3500–6500 ft): In step 2, after pressing dough in bottom of pan and sealing perforations, bake 3 minutes.

1 Bar: Calories 90 (Calories from Fat 35); Total Fat 4g (Saturated Fat 2g; Trans Fat 0g); Cholesterol 5mg; Sodium 60mg; Total Carbohydrate 12g (Dietary Fiber 0g; Sugars 9g); Protein 1g **% Daily Value:** Vitamin A 0%; Vitamin C 0%; Calcium 2%; Iron 0% **Exchanges:** 1 Other Carbohydrate, 1 Fat **Carbohydrate Choices:** 1

rocky road fudge bars

48 BARS

PREP TIME: *25 minutes*
START TO FINISH: *2 hours*

MARY WILSON
Leesburg, GA
Bake-Off® Contest 23, 1972

1 Heat oven to 350°F. Grease 13 × 9-inch pan with shortening or cooking spray; lightly flour. In 2-quart saucepan, melt ½ cup butter and 1 oz baking chocolate over low heat, stirring until smooth. Remove from heat. Stir in 1 cup flour and remaining base ingredients until well mixed. Spread in pan.

2 In small bowl, beat 6 oz cream cheese, ¼ cup butter, ½ cup granulated sugar, 2 tablespoons flour, ½ teaspoon vanilla and 1 egg with electric mixer on medium speed 1 minute, scraping bowl occasionally, until smooth and fluffy. Stir in ¼ cup nuts. Spread over chocolate mixture; sprinkle evenly with chocolate chips.

3 Bake 25 to 35 minutes or until toothpick inserted in center comes out clean. Immediately sprinkle with marshmallows. Bake 2 minutes longer.

4 While marshmallows are baking, in 3-quart saucepan, cook remaining 2 oz cream cheese, ¼ cup butter, the milk and 1 oz baking chocolate over low heat, stirring until well blended. Remove from heat. Stir in powdered sugar and 1 teaspoon vanilla until smooth. Immediately pour frosting over puffed marshmallows and lightly swirl with knife to marble. Refrigerate until firm, about 1 hour. For bars, cut into 8 rows by 6 rows. Store in refrigerator.

High Altitude (3500–6500 ft): No change.

BASE

½ cup butter or margarine

1 oz unsweetened baking chocolate, cut into pieces

1 cup Pillsbury BEST® all-purpose flour

1 cup granulated sugar

1 teaspoon baking powder

1 teaspoon vanilla

2 eggs

¾ cup chopped nuts

FILLING

6 oz cream cheese (from 8-oz package), softened

¼ cup butter or margarine, softened

½ cup granulated sugar

2 tablespoons Pillsbury BEST® all-purpose flour

½ teaspoon vanilla

1 egg

¼ cup chopped nuts

1 cup semisweet chocolate chips (6 oz)

2 cups miniature marshmallows

FROSTING

Remaining 2 oz cream cheese (from 8-oz package)

¼ cup butter or margarine

¼ cup milk

1 oz unsweetened baking chocolate, cut into pieces

3 cups powdered sugar

1 teaspoon vanilla

1 Bar: Calories 170 (Calories from Fat 80); Total Fat 9g (Saturated Fat 5g; Trans Fat 0g); Cholesterol 30mg; Sodium 60mg; Total Carbohydrate 21g (Dietary Fiber 0g; Sugars 17g); Protein 2g **% Daily Value:** Vitamin A 4%; Vitamin C 0%; Calcium 0%; Iron 4% **Exchanges:** ½ Starch, 1 Other Carbohydrate, 1½ Fat **Carbohydrate Choices:** 1½

by cracky bars

MISS YVONNE M. WHYTE
New Bedford, MA
Bake-Off® Contest 04, 1952

36 BARS

PREP TIME: *25 minutes*
START TO FINISH: *1 hour 45 minutes*

1¾ cups Pillsbury BEST®
  all-purpose flour
1 teaspoon salt
¼ teaspoon baking soda
1 cup sugar
¾ cup shortening
1 teaspoon vanilla
2 eggs
⅓ cup milk
1 oz unsweetened baking
  chocolate, melted
¾ cup chopped walnuts
9 double graham crackers
¾ cup semisweet chocolate chips

1 Heat oven to 375°F. Grease 13 × 9-inch pan with shortening or cooking spray. In small bowl, stir together flour, salt and baking soda; set aside.

2 In large bowl, beat sugar, shortening, vanilla and eggs with electric mixer on medium speed, scraping bowl occasionally, until well blended. Beat in flour mixture alternately with milk until well blended.

3 Place ⅓ of batter in medium bowl. Stir in melted chocolate and walnuts. Spread chocolate batter in pan.

4 Arrange graham cracker squares over batter in pan. To remaining ⅔ of batter, stir in chocolate chips. Drop batter by spoonfuls over graham crackers; spread to cover.

5 Bake 23 to 28 minutes or until edges are light golden brown. Cool completely in pan on cooling rack, about 1 hour. For bars, cut into 6 rows by 6 rows.

High Altitude (3500–6500 ft): No change.

1 Bar: Calories 140 (Calories from Fat 70); Total Fat 8g (Saturated Fat 2.5g; Trans Fat 1g); Cholesterol 10mg; Sodium 100mg; Total Carbohydrate 16g (Dietary Fiber 0g; Sugars 9g); Protein 2g **% Daily Value:** Vitamin A 0%; Vitamin C 0%; Calcium 0%; Iron 4% **Exchanges:** ½ Starch, ½ Other Carbohydrate, 1½ Fat **Carbohydrate Choices:** 1

peanut blossoms

4 DOZEN COOKIES

PREP TIME: *1 hour*

START TO FINISH: *1 hour*

FREDA SMITH
Gibsonburg, OH
Bake-Off® Contest 09, 1957

1 Heat oven to 375°F. In large bowl, beat flour, ½ cup granulated sugar, the brown sugar, baking soda, salt, shortening, peanut butter, milk, vanilla and egg with electric mixer on low speed, scraping bowl occasionally, until stiff dough forms.

2 Shape dough into 1-inch balls; roll in granulated sugar. Place 2 inches apart on ungreased cookie sheets.

3 Bake 10 to 12 minutes or until golden brown. Immediately top each cookie with 1 milk chocolate candy, pressing down firmly so cookie cracks around edge. Remove from cookie sheets.

High Altitude (3500–6500 ft): No change.

1¾ cups Pillsbury BEST®
 all-purpose flour
½ cup granulated sugar
½ cup packed brown sugar
1 teaspoon baking soda
½ teaspoon salt
½ cup shortening
½ cup peanut butter
2 tablespoons milk
1 teaspoon vanilla
1 egg
Granulated sugar
48 milk chocolate candy drops or
 pieces, unwrapped

1 Cookie: Calories 100 (Calories from Fat 45); Total Fat 5g (Saturated Fat 1.5g; Trans Fat 0g); Cholesterol 5mg; Sodium 70mg; Total Carbohydrate 12g (Dietary Fiber 0g; Sugars 8g); Protein 2g **% Daily Value:** Vitamin A 0%; Vitamin C 0%; Calcium 0%; Iron 2% **Exchanges:** 1 Other Carbohydrate, 1 Fat **Carbohydrate Choices:** 1

peanut butter–brownie cookies

DEB MCGOWAN
Louisville, OH
Bake-Off® Contest 41, 2004

2 DOZEN COOKIES

PREP TIME: *1 hour*
START TO FINISH: *1 hour 30 minutes*

1 box (19.5 oz) Pillsbury® traditional fudge brownie mix

¼ cup butter or margarine, melted

4 oz cream cheese (half of 8-oz package), softened

1 egg

1 cup powdered sugar

1 cup creamy peanut butter

½ container (1-lb size) Pillsbury® Creamy Supreme® chocolate fudge frosting (about ¾ cup)

1 Heat oven to 350°F. In medium bowl, beat brownie mix, melted butter, cream cheese and egg 50 strokes with spoon until well blended (dough will be sticky).

2 Drop dough by rounded tablespoonfuls 2 inches apart onto ungreased cookie sheets to make 24 cookies; smooth edge of each to form round cookie.

3 In small bowl, mix powdered sugar and peanut butter with spoon until mixture forms a ball. With hands, roll rounded teaspoonfuls peanut butter mixture into 24 balls. Lightly press 1 ball into center of each ball of dough.

4 Bake 10 to 14 minutes or until edges are set. Cool cookies on cookie sheets at least 30 minutes.

5 Remove cooled cookies from cookie sheets. Spread thin layer of frosting over peanut butter portion of each.

High Altitude (3500–6500 ft): Before baking, flatten cookies slightly. Bake 11 to 15 minutes.

1 Cookie: Calories 270 (Calories from Fat 120); Total Fat 13g (Saturated Fat 6g; Trans Fat 0g); Cholesterol 20mg; Sodium 140mg; Total Carbohydrate 32g (Dietary Fiber 1g; Sugars 24g); Protein 4g **% Daily Value:** Vitamin A 2%; Vitamin C 0%; Calcium 0%; Iron 8% **Exchanges:** ½ Starch, 1½ Other Carbohydrate, ½ High-Fat Meat, 2 Fat **Carbohydrate Choices:** 2

so-easy sugar cookies

MRS. KATHRYN BLACKBURN
National Park, NJ
Bake-Off® Contest 30, 1982

4 DOZEN COOKIES

PREP TIME: *15 minutes*
START TO FINISH: *35 minutes*

¾ cup sugar

⅓ cup butter or margarine, softened,
   or shortening

⅓ cup vegetable oil

1 tablespoon milk

1 to 2 teaspoons almond extract

1 egg

1½ cups Pillsbury BEST®
   all-purpose flour

1½ teaspoons baking powder

¼ teaspoon salt

1 tablespoon regular or colored sugar

1 Heat oven to 375°F. In large bowl, beat ¾ cup sugar, the butter, oil, milk, almond extract and egg with electric mixer on medium speed, scraping bowl occasionally, until light and fluffy. On low speed, beat in flour, baking powder and salt until well blended. Spread evenly in ungreased 15 × 10 × 1-inch pan. Sprinkle with 1 tablespoon sugar.

2 Bake 10 to 12 minutes or until light golden brown. Cool 5 minutes. Cut diagonally into diamond-shaped cookies or into 8 rows by 6 rows to make 48 square cookies.

FOOD PROCESSOR DIRECTIONS: In food processor, place ¾ cup sugar, the butter, oil, milk, almond extract and egg. Cover; process until light and fluffy. Add flour, baking powder and salt. Cover; process with on/off pulses just until flour is well blended (do not overprocess or cookies will be tough). Continue as directed above.

High Altitude (3500–6500 ft): Decrease baking powder to 1 teaspoon.

1 Cookie: Calories 50 (Calories from Fat 25); Total Fat 3g (Saturated Fat 1g; Trans Fat 0g); Cholesterol 10mg; Sodium 40mg; Total Carbohydrate 6g (Dietary Fiber 0g; Sugars 3g); Protein 0g **% Daily Value:** Vitamin A 0%; Vitamin C 0%; Calcium 0%; Iron 0% **Exchanges:** ½ Other Carbohydrate, ½ Fat **Carbohydrate Choices:** ½

cherry winks

5 DOZEN COOKIES

PREP TIME: *1 hour 20 minutes*
START TO FINISH: *1 hour 20 minutes*

RUTH DEROUSSEAU
Rice Lake, WI
Bake-Off® Contest 02, 1950

1 In large bowl, beat sugar and shortening with electric mixer on medium speed, scraping bowl occasionally, until well blended. Beat in milk, vanilla and eggs. On low speed, beat in flour, baking powder, baking soda and salt, scraping bowl occasionally, until dough forms. Stir in pecans, dates and ⅓ cup chopped cherries. If necessary, cover with plastic wrap and refrigerate 15 minutes for easier handling.

2 Heat oven to 375°F. Grease cookie sheets with shortening or cooking spray. Drop dough by rounded teaspoonfuls into cereal; coat thoroughly. Shape into balls. Place 2 inches apart on cookie sheets. Lightly press maraschino cherry quarter into top of each ball.

3 Bake 10 to 15 minutes or until light golden brown.

High Altitude (3500–6500 ft): No change.

1 cup sugar

¾ cup shortening

2 tablespoons milk

1 teaspoon vanilla

2 eggs

2¼ cups Pillsbury BEST®
   all-purpose flour

1 teaspoon baking powder

½ teaspoon baking soda

½ teaspoon salt

1 cup chopped pecans

1 cup chopped dates

⅓ cup chopped maraschino cherries,
   well drained*

1½ cups coarsely crushed corn
   flakes cereal

15 maraschino cherries, quartered

1 Cookie: Calories 80 (Calories from Fat 35); Total Fat 4g (Saturated Fat 1g; Trans Fat 0g); Cholesterol 5mg; Sodium 45mg; Total Carbohydrate 11g (Dietary Fiber 0g; Sugars 6g); Protein 1g **% Daily Value:** Vitamin A 0%; Vitamin C 0%; Calcium 0%; Iron 2% **Exchanges:** ½ Other Carbohydrate, 1 Fat **Carbohydrate Choices:** 1

*Chop the maraschino cherries then drain them on paper towels to eliminate excess moisture.

caramel-filled chocolate cookies

JEAN OLSON
Wallingford, IA
Bake-Off® Contest 34, 1990

4 DOZEN COOKIES

PREP TIME: *1 hour*
START TO FINISH: *1 hour 30 minutes*

2½ cups Pillsbury BEST®
   all-purpose flour

¾ cup unsweetened baking cocoa

1 teaspoon baking soda

1 cup granulated sugar

1 cup packed brown sugar

1 cup butter or margarine, softened

2 teaspoons vanilla

2 eggs

1 cup chopped pecans

1 tablespoon granulated sugar

48 round chewy caramels in milk
   chocolate (from 12-oz bag),
   unwrapped

4 oz vanilla-flavored candy coating
   (almond bark), if desired

1   In small bowl, stir together flour, cocoa and baking soda; set aside. In large bowl, beat 1 cup granulated sugar, the brown sugar and butter with electric mixer on medium speed, scraping bowl occasionally, until light and fluffy. Beat in vanilla and eggs. On low speed, beat in flour mixture until well blended. Stir in ½ cup of the pecans. If necessary, cover with plastic wrap and refrigerate 30 minutes for easier handling.

2   Heat oven to 375°F. In small bowl, mix remaining ½ cup pecans and 1 tablespoon sugar. With floured hands, shape about 1 tablespoon dough around each caramel, covering completely. Press one side of each ball into pecan mixture. Place nut side up 2 inches apart on ungreased cookie sheets.

3   Bake 7 to 10 minutes or until set and slightly cracked. Cool 2 minutes; remove from cookie sheets to cooling racks. Cool completely, about 15 minutes.

4   In 1-quart saucepan, melt candy coating over low heat, stirring constantly until smooth. Drizzle over cookies.

High Altitude (3500–6500 ft): Increase all-purpose flour to 2¾ cups.

1 Cookie: Calories 150 (Calories from Fat 60); Total Fat 7g (Saturated Fat 3.5g; Trans Fat 0g); Cholesterol 20mg; Sodium 70mg; Total Carbohydrate 19g (Dietary Fiber 0g; Sugars 13g); Protein 2g **% Daily Value:** Vitamin A 2%; Vitamin C 0%; Calcium 0%; Iron 4% **Exchanges:** ½ Starch, ½ Other Carbohydrate, 1½ Fat **Carbohydrate Choices:** 1

german chocolate thumbprint cookies

5 DOZEN COOKIES

PREP TIME: *1 hour*

START TO FINISH: *1 hour 20 minutes*

FRANCES SHEPPARD
Corsicana, TX
Bake-Off® Contest 34, 1990

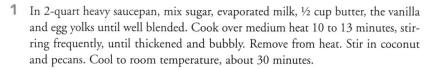

1   In 2-quart heavy saucepan, mix sugar, evaporated milk, ½ cup butter, the vanilla and egg yolks until well blended. Cook over medium heat 10 to 13 minutes, stirring frequently, until thickened and bubbly. Remove from heat. Stir in coconut and pecans. Cool to room temperature, about 30 minutes.

2   Reserve 1¼ cups of the topping mixture; set aside. In large bowl, stir cookie ingredients and remaining topping mixture with spoon until thoroughly moistened. Cover with plastic wrap; refrigerate 30 minutes for easier handling.

3   Heat oven to 350°F. Shape dough into 1-inch balls. Place 2 inches apart on ungreased cookie sheets. With thumb, make an indentation in center of each ball. Fill each indentation with rounded ½ teaspoon reserved topping mixture.

4   Bake 10 to 13 minutes or until set. Cool 5 minutes; remove from cookie sheets.

High Altitude (3500–6500 ft): Add ¼ cup all-purpose flour to dry cake mix.

TOPPING

1 cup sugar

1 cup evaporated milk

½ cup unsalted butter, butter or margarine, softened

1 teaspoon vanilla

3 egg yolks, beaten

1½ cups flaked coconut

1½ cups chopped pecans

COOKIES

1 box (18.25 oz) Pillsbury® Moist Supreme® German chocolate cake mix

⅓ cup unsalted butter, butter or margarine, melted

1 Cookie: Calories 110 (Calories from Fat 60); Total Fat 6g (Saturated Fat 3g; Trans Fat 0g); Cholesterol 20mg; Sodium 75mg; Total Carbohydrate 12g (Dietary Fiber 0g; Sugars 9g); Protein 1g **% Daily Value:** Vitamin A 2%; Vitamin C 0%; Calcium 2%; Iron 0% **Exchanges:** 1 Other Carbohydrate, 1 Fat **Carbohydrate Choices:** 1

starlight mint surprise cookies

LAURA ROTT

Naperville, IL

Bake-Off® Contest 01, 1949

5 DOZEN COOKIES

PREP TIME: *1 hour*

START TO FINISH: *3 hours*

1 cup granulated sugar

½ cup packed brown sugar

¾ cup butter or margarine, softened

2 tablespoons water

1 teaspoon vanilla

2 eggs

3 cups Pillsbury BEST® all-purpose flour

1 teaspoon baking soda

½ teaspoon salt

60 thin rectangular crème de menthe chocolate candies (from three 4.67-oz packages), unwrapped

60 walnut halves or pieces

1 In large bowl, beat sugars, butter, water, vanilla and eggs with electric mixer on medium speed, scraping bowl occasionally, until blended. On low speed, beat in flour, baking soda and salt until well blended. Cover with plastic wrap; refrigerate at least 2 hours for easier handling.

2 Heat oven to 375°F. Using about 1 tablespoon dough, press dough around each chocolate candy to cover completely. Place 2 inches apart on ungreased cookie sheets. Top each with walnut half.

3 Bake 7 to 9 minutes or until light golden brown. Immediately remove from cookie sheets.

High Altitude (3500–6500 ft): No change.

1 Cookie: Calories 110 (Calories from Fat 45); Total Fat 5g (Saturated Fat 2.5g; Trans Fat 0g); Cholesterol 15mg; Sodium 65mg; Total Carbohydrate 13g (Dietary Fiber 0g; Sugars 8g); Protein 2g **% Daily Value:** Vitamin A 0%; Vitamin C 0%; Calcium 0%; Iron 2% **Exchanges:** 1 Other Carbohydrate, 1 Fat **Carbohydrate Choices:** 1

snappy turtle cookies

BEATRICE HARLIB
Lincolnwood, IL
Bake-Off® Contest 04, 1952

3½ DOZEN COOKIES

PREP TIME: *1 hour 30 minutes*
START TO FINISH: *2 hours 45 minutes*

COOKIES

½ cup packed brown sugar

½ cup butter or margarine, softened

¼ teaspoon vanilla

⅛ teaspoon maple flavor, if desired

1 egg

1 egg, separated

1½ cups Pillsbury BEST®
all-purpose flour

¼ teaspoon baking soda

¼ teaspoon salt

1 cup pecan halves, each broken
lengthwise into 2 pieces

FROSTING

⅓ cup semisweet chocolate chips

3 tablespoons milk

1 tablespoon butter or margarine

1 cup powdered sugar

1 In large bowl, beat brown sugar and ½ cup butter with electric mixer on medium speed, scraping bowl occasionally, until light and fluffy. Beat in vanilla, maple flavor, 1 whole egg and 1 egg yolk until well blended. On low speed, beat in flour, baking soda and salt. Cover with plastic wrap; refrigerate at least 1 hour for easier handling.

2 Heat oven to 350°F. Grease cookie sheets with shortening or cooking spray. Arrange pecan pieces in groups of 5 on cookie sheets to resemble head and legs of turtle. In small bowl, beat egg white with fork or wire whisk. Shape dough into 1-inch balls. Dip bottoms in beaten egg white; press lightly onto pecans (tips of pecans should show).

3 Bake 10 to 12 minutes or until edges are light golden brown. Immediately remove from cookie sheets to cooling racks. Cool completely, about 15 minutes.

4 Meanwhile, in 1-quart saucepan, heat chocolate chips, milk and 1 tablespoon butter over low heat, stirring constantly, until chips are melted and mixture is smooth. Remove from heat. Stir in powdered sugar. If necessary, add additional powdered sugar until frosting is spreadable. Frost cooled cookies. Let frosting set before storing in tightly covered container.

High Altitude (3500–6500 ft): No change.

1 Cookie: Calories 90 (Calories from Fat 45); Total Fat 5g (Saturated Fat 2g; Trans Fat 0g); Cholesterol 15mg; Sodium 45mg; Total Carbohydrate 10g (Dietary Fiber 0g; Sugars 6g); Protein 1g **% Daily Value:** Vitamin A 0%; Vitamin C 0%; Calcium 0%; Iron 2% **Exchanges:** 1 Other Carbohydrate, 1 Fat **Carbohydrate Choices:** ½

candy bar cookies

40 COOKIES

PREP TIME: *1 hour 15 minutes*

START TO FINISH: *1 hour 15 minutes*

ALICE REESE
Minneapolis, MN
Bake-Off® Contest 13, 1961

1 In large bowl, mix all base ingredients except flour with spoon until well blended. Stir in flour until dough forms. If necessary, cover dough with plastic wrap and refrigerate 1 hour for easier handling.

2 Heat oven to 325°F. On well-floured surface, roll out half of dough at a time into 10 × 8-inch rectangle. With pastry wheel or knife, cut into 2-inch squares. Place ½ inch apart on ungreased cookie sheets.

3 Bake 10 to 13 minutes or until set. Immediately remove from cookie sheets to cooling racks. Cool completely, about 15 minutes.

4 In 2-quart saucepan, heat caramels, 3 tablespoons whipping cream and 3 tablespoons butter over low heat, stirring frequently, until caramels are melted and mixture is smooth. Remove from heat. Stir in ¾ cup powdered sugar and the chopped pecans (add additional whipping cream a few drops at a time if needed for desired spreading consistency). Spread 1 teaspoon warm filling on each cookie square.

5 In 1-quart saucepan, heat chocolate chips, 1 tablespoon whipping cream and 2 teaspoons butter over low heat, stirring frequently, until chips are melted and mixture is smooth. REMOVE FROM HEAT. Stir in 3 tablespoons powdered sugar and 1 teaspoon vanilla. Spread glaze evenly over caramel filling on each cookie. Top each with pecan half.

High Altitude (3500–6500 ft): No change.

BASE

¾ cup powdered sugar

¾ cup butter or margarine, softened

2 tablespoons whipping cream

1 teaspoon vanilla

2 cups Pillsbury BEST® all-purpose flour

FILLING

21 caramels, unwrapped

3 tablespoons whipping cream

3 tablespoons butter or margarine

¾ cup powdered sugar

¾ cup chopped pecans

GLAZE

⅓ cup semisweet chocolate chips

1 tablespoon whipping cream

2 teaspoons butter or margarine

3 tablespoons powdered sugar

1 teaspoon vanilla

40 pecan halves (½ cup), if desired

1 Cookie: Calories 130 (Calories from Fat 70); Total Fat 8g (Saturated Fat 4g; Trans Fat 0g); Cholesterol 15mg; Sodium 45mg; Total Carbohydrate 15g (Dietary Fiber 0g; Sugars 8g); Protein 1g **% Daily Value:** Vitamin A 4%; Vitamin C 0%; Calcium 0%; Iron 2% **Exchanges:** ½ Starch, ½ Other Carbohydrate, 1½ Fat **Carbohydrate Choices:** 1

funfetti cookies

MOLLY TAYLOR
Maryville, TN
Bake-Off® Contest 34, 1990

3 DOZEN COOKIES

PREP TIME: *40 minutes*
START TO FINISH: *40 minutes*

1 box (18.9 oz) Pillsbury® Moist Supreme® Funfetti® cake mix

⅓ cup vegetable oil

2 eggs

½ container (15.6-oz size) Pillsbury® Creamy Supreme® Funfetti® pink frosting

1 Heat oven to 375°F. In large bowl, mix cake mix, oil and eggs with spoon until thoroughly moistened. Shape dough into 1-inch balls. Place 2 inches apart on ungreased cookie sheets. With bottom of glass dipped in flour, flatten balls to ¼-inch thickness.

2 Bake 6 to 8 minutes or until edges are light golden brown. Cool 1 minute; remove from cookie sheets.

3 Spread frosting over warm cookies. Immediately sprinkle each with candy bits from frosting. Let frosting set before storing in tightly covered container.

High Altitude (3500–6500 ft): Add ½ cup all-purpose flour to dry cake mix.

1 Cookie: Calories 110 (Calories from Fat 40); Total Fat 4.5g (Saturated Fat 1.5g; Trans Fat 0g); Cholesterol 10mg; Sodium 105mg; Total Carbohydrate 16g (Dietary Fiber 0g; Sugars 13g); Protein 0g **% Daily Value:** Vitamin A 0%; Vitamin C 0%; Calcium 0%; Iron 0% **Exchanges:** 1 Other Carbohydrate, 1 Fat **Carbohydrate Choices:** 1

fudgy bonbons

MARY ANNE TYNDALL
Whiteville, NC
Bake-Off® Contest 36, 1994

5 DOZEN COOKIES

PREP TIME: *1 hour 10 minutes*
START TO FINISH: *1 hour 10 minutes*

1 bag (12 oz) semisweet chocolate chips (2 cups)

¼ cup butter or margarine

1 can (14 oz) sweetened condensed milk (not evaporated)

2 cups Pillsbury BEST® all-purpose flour

½ cup finely chopped nuts, if desired

1 teaspoon vanilla

60 milk chocolate candy drops or pieces, unwrapped

2 oz white baking bar or vanilla-flavored candy coating (almond bark)

1 teaspoon shortening or vegetable oil

1 Heat oven to 350°F. In 2-quart saucepan, heat chocolate chips and butter over very low heat, stirring frequently, until chips are melted and smooth. Stir in sweetened condensed milk (mixture will be stiff).

2 In medium bowl, mix flour, nuts, chocolate mixture and vanilla with spoon until dough forms. Shape 1 measuring tablespoon dough around each milk chocolate candy, covering completely. Place 1 inch apart on ungreased cookie sheets.

3 Bake 6 to 8 minutes (do not overbake). Cookies will be soft and appear shiny but will become firm as they cool. Immediately remove from cookie sheets to cooling racks. Cool completely, about 15 minutes.

4 In 1-quart saucepan, heat white baking bar and shortening over low heat, stirring occasionally, until melted and smooth. Drizzle over cookies. Let set before storing in tightly covered container.

High Altitude (3500–6500 ft): Increase all-purpose flour to 2¼ cups.

1 Cookie: Calories 100 (Calories from Fat 45); Total Fat 5g (Saturated Fat 2.5g; Trans Fat 0g); Cholesterol 5mg; Sodium 20mg; Total Carbohydrate 14g (Dietary Fiber 0g; Sugars 10g); Protein 2g **% Daily Value:** Vitamin A 0%; Vitamin C 0%; Calcium 4%; Iron 2% **Exchanges:** 1 Other Carbohydrate, 1 Fat **Carbohydrate Choices:** 1

Caramel-Pecan Sticky Bun Cookies (page 51) ►

ginger cookie capers

PATTY ROSE WELTI
Plainview, MN
Bake-Off® Contest 06, 1954

2 DOZEN (4-INCH) COOKIES

PREP TIME: *50 minutes*
START TO FINISH: *2 hours 50 minutes*

2 cups Pillsbury BEST® all-purpose flour
½ cup shortening
½ cup molasses
⅓ cup sugar
3 tablespoons hot water
1 teaspoon baking powder
1 teaspoon ground cinnamon
½ teaspoon ground ginger
¼ teaspoon baking soda

1   Heat oven to 400°F. In large bowl, beat all ingredients with electric mixer on medium speed, scraping bowl occasionally, until well blended. Cover with plastic wrap; refrigerate at least 2 hours for easier handling.

2   On floured surface, roll half of dough at a time to ⅛-inch thickness. Cut with gingerbread man cutter. On ungreased cookie sheets, place cutouts 1 inch apart.

3   Bake 7 to 9 minutes or until set. Remove from cookie sheets; cool completely before decorating.

High Altitude (3500–6500 ft): No change.

1 Cookie: Calories 110 (Calories from Fat 40); Total Fat 4.5g (Saturated Fat 1g; Trans Fat 0.5g); Cholesterol 0mg; Sodium 35mg; Total Carbohydrate 16g (Dietary Fiber 0g; Sugars 7g); Protein 1g **% Daily Value:** Vitamin A 0%; Vitamin C 0%; Calcium 2%; Iron 4% **Exchanges:** 1 Other Carbohydrate, 1 Fat **Carbohydrate Choices:** 1

white chocolate chunk cookies

5 DOZEN COOKIES

PREP TIME: *1 hour 15 minutes*

START TO FINISH: *1 hour 15 minutes*

DOTTIE DUE
Edgewood, KY
Bake-Off® Contest 33, 1988

1 Heat oven to 350°F. In large bowl, beat sugars and shortening with electric mixer on medium speed, scraping bowl occasionally, until light and fluffy. Add eggs, one at a time, beating well after each addition. Beat in vanilla. On low speed, beat in flour, baking powder, baking soda and salt until well blended. Stir in remaining ingredients.

2 Onto ungreased cookie sheets, drop dough by rounded tablespoonfuls 2 inches apart.

3 Bake 10 to 15 minutes or until light golden brown. Cool 1 minute; remove from cookie sheets.

High Altitude (3500–6500 ft): Heat oven to 375°F. Decrease baking powder and baking soda to ½ teaspoon each. Bake 8 to 12 minutes.

¾ cup granulated sugar

¾ cup packed brown sugar

1 cup shortening

3 eggs

1 teaspoon vanilla

2½ cups Pillsbury BEST® all-purpose flour

1 teaspoon baking powder

1 teaspoon baking soda

½ teaspoon salt

1 cup coconut

½ cup old-fashioned or quick-cooking oats

½ cup chopped walnuts

2 packages (6 oz each) white chocolate baking bars, cut into ¼- to ½-inch chunks

1 Cookie: Calories 120 (Calories from Fat 60); Total Fat 7g (Saturated Fat 2.5g; Trans Fat 0.5g); Cholesterol 10mg; Sodium 60mg; Total Carbohydrate 14g (Dietary Fiber 0g; Sugars 9g); Protein 1g **% Daily Value:** Vitamin A 0%; Vitamin C 0%; Calcium 2%; Iron 2% **Exchanges:** 1 Other Carbohydrate, 1½ Fat **Carbohydrate Choices:** 1

chocolate nutbutter cookies

MRS. MARVIN J. DUNCAN
Washington, D.C.
Bake-Off® Contest 03, 1951

4 DOZEN COOKIES
PREP TIME: *55 minutes*
START TO FINISH: *55 minutes*

1¼ cups sugar

½ cup shortening

½ cup chunky or creamy peanut butter

1½ teaspoons vanilla

2 eggs

2 cups Pillsbury BEST® all-purpose flour

½ cup unsweetened baking cocoa

2 teaspoons baking powder

½ teaspoon salt

⅓ cup milk

1 Heat oven to 400°F. In large bowl, beat sugar, shortening and peanut butter with electric mixer on medium speed, scraping bowl occasionally, until light and fluffy. Beat in vanilla and eggs.

2 In medium bowl, stir together flour, cocoa, baking powder and salt. Beat into sugar mixture alternately with milk.

3 Onto ungreased cookie sheets, drop dough by rounded teaspoonfuls. Flatten in crisscross pattern with fork dipped in flour.

4 Bake 6 to 10 minutes or until bottoms are light brown.

High Altitude (3500–6500 ft): No change.

1 Cookie: Calories 80 (Calories from Fat 35); Total Fat 4g (Saturated Fat 1g; Trans Fat 0g); Cholesterol 10mg; Sodium 60mg; Total Carbohydrate 10g (Dietary Fiber 0g; Sugars 6g); Protein 2g **% Daily Value:** Vitamin A 0%; Vitamin C 0%; Calcium 0%; Iron 2% **Exchanges:** ½ Other Carbohydrate, 1 Fat **Carbohydrate Choices:** ½

maple-oat chewies

KITTY CAHILL
St. Paul, MN
Bake-Off® Contest 32, 1986

5 DOZEN COOKIES

PREP TIME: *1 hour 30 minutes*
START TO FINISH: *1 hour 30 minutes*

1 cup granulated sugar

1 cup packed brown sugar

1 cup butter or margarine, softened

1 tablespoon molasses

2 teaspoons maple flavor

2 eggs

1¾ cups Pillsbury BEST®
all-purpose flour

2 teaspoons baking powder

1 teaspoon ground cinnamon

½ teaspoon salt

2 cups quick-cooking or
old-fashioned oats

2 cups crisp rice cereal

1 Heat oven to 350°F. Grease cookie sheets with shortening or cooking spray. In large bowl, beat sugars and butter with electric mixer on medium speed, scraping bowl occasionally, until light and fluffy. Beat in molasses, maple flavor and eggs. Add flour, baking powder, cinnamon and salt; beat on medium speed until well blended. Stir in oats and cereal.

2 Onto cookie sheets, drop dough by heaping teaspoonfuls 2 inches apart.

3 Bake 8 to 12 minutes or until light golden brown. Cool 2 minutes; remove from cookie sheets.

High Altitude (3500–6500 ft): No change.

1 Cookie: Calories 90 (Calories from Fat 30); Total Fat 3.5g (Saturated Fat 2g; Trans Fat 0g); Cholesterol 15mg; Sodium 60mg; Total Carbohydrate 12g (Dietary Fiber 0g; Sugars 7g); Protein 1g **% Daily Value:** Vitamin A 2%; Vitamin C 0%; Calcium 0%; Iron 4% **Exchanges:** 1 Other Carbohydrate, ½ Fat **Carbohydrate Choices:** 1

cinnamon-toffee-pecan cookies

JENNIFER MEYER
Elmwood Park, IL
Bake-Off® Contest 39, 2000

2 DOZEN COOKIES

PREP TIME: *50 minutes*

START TO FINISH: *50 minutes*

1 roll (16.5 oz) Pillsbury® Create 'n Bake™ refrigerated sugar cookies

2 teaspoons ground cinnamon

½ teaspoon ground nutmeg

2 teaspoons vanilla

¾ cup chopped pecans

½ cup toffee bits

1 Heat oven to 350°F. Spray cookie sheets with cooking spray. In large bowl, break up cookie dough. Stir in cinnamon, nutmeg and vanilla until well mixed. Stir in pecans and toffee bits until well mixed.

2 Onto cookie sheets, drop dough by heaping teaspoonfuls 3 inches apart.

3 Bake 11 to 14 minutes or until edges are golden brown. Cool 3 minutes; remove from cookie sheets.

High Altitude (3500°6500 ft): Bake 12 to 15 minutes.

1 Cookie: Calories 150 (Calories from Fat 80); Total Fat 9g (Saturated Fat 2.5g; Trans Fat 1g); Cholesterol 15mg; Sodium 65mg; Total Carbohydrate 17g (Dietary Fiber 0g; Sugars 12g); Protein 1g **% Daily Value:** Vitamin A 0%; Vitamin C 0%; Calcium 0%; Iron 2% **Exchanges:** 1 Other Carbohydrate, 2 Fat **Carbohydrate Choices:** 1

milk chocolate–butterscotch café cookies

9 LARGE COOKIES

PREP TIME: *40 minutes*

START TO FINISH: *40 minutes*

CINDY SCHMUELLING

Fort Mitchell, KY

Bake-Off® Contest 40, 2002

1 Heat oven to 350°F. Spray 1 large or 2 small cookie sheets with cooking spray. In large bowl, break up cookie dough. Stir in brown sugar and vanilla. Stir in oats, butterscotch chips and chocolate. (Dough will be stiff.)

2 Onto cookie sheets, drop dough by rounded ¼ cupfuls 2 inches apart. Flatten each with fingers to ½-inch thickness.

3 Bake 13 to 18 minutes or until cookies are slightly puffed and edges are golden brown. Cool 1 minute; remove from cookie sheets.

High Altitude (3500–6500 ft): No change.

1 roll (16.5 oz) Pillsbury® Create 'n Bake™ refrigerated sugar cookies

⅓ cup packed brown sugar

1 teaspoon vanilla

¾ cup old-fashioned oats

½ cup butterscotch chips

2 bars (1.55 oz each) milk chocolate candy, unwrapped, chopped

1 Large Cookie: Calories 390 (Calories from Fat 150); Total Fat 17g (Saturated Fat 6g; Trans Fat 2.5g); Cholesterol 20mg; Sodium 160mg; Total Carbohydrate 57g (Dietary Fiber 0g; Sugars 37g); Protein 4g **% Daily Value:** Vitamin A 0%; Vitamin C 0%; Calcium 4%; Iron 8% **Exchanges:** 1 Starch, 3 Other Carbohydrate, 3 Fat **Carbohydrate Choices:** 4

coconut islands·

SISTER MARIA JOSE CANNON
Honolulu, HI
Bake-Off® Contest 05, 1953

ABOUT 3½ DOZEN COOKIES
PREP TIME: *1 hour 20 minutes*
START TO FINISH: *1 hour 20 minutes*

COOKIES

3 oz unsweetened baking
    chocolate, chopped
¼ cup hot brewed coffee
2 cups Pillsbury BEST® all-purpose flour
½ teaspoon salt
½ teaspoon baking soda
½ cup shortening
1 cup packed brown sugar
1 egg
⅔ cup sour cream
⅓ cup flaked coconut

FROSTING

1½ oz unsweetened baking chocolate,
    chopped
¼ cup sour cream
1 tablespoon butter or margarine
1½ to 2 cups powdered sugar
1 to 2 teaspoons cold brewed coffee

GARNISH

1 cup flaked coconut

1 Heat oven to 375°F. Grease large cookie sheets with shortening or cooking spray. In 1-quart saucepan, melt 3 oz chocolate in hot coffee over low heat, stirring frequently; cool. Meanwhile, in small bowl, stir together flour, salt and baking soda; set aside.

2 In large bowl, beat shortening and brown sugar with electric mixer on medium speed, scraping bowl occasionally, until well blended. Beat in egg and chocolate mixture. Beat in ⅔ cup sour cream alternately with the flour mixture until well blended. Stir in ⅓ cup coconut.

3 Onto cookie sheets, drop dough by heaping teaspoonfuls about 2 inches apart.

4 Bake 10 to 12 minutes or until set. Meanwhile, in 1½-quart heavy saucepan, heat 1½ oz chocolate, ¼ cup sour cream and the butter, stirring constantly, until chocolate is melted. Immediately remove from heat. Gradually stir in enough powdered sugar until frosting is spreadable. If necessary, thin with coffee or water, a few drops at a time.

5 Remove cookies from cookie sheets to cooling racks; cool about 2 minutes. Spread cookies with frosting. Sprinkle tops with 1 cup coconut. Store in tightly covered container.

High Altitude (3500®6500 ft): Bake 9 to 11 minutes.

1 Cookie: Calories 130 (Calories from Fat 60); Total Fat 6g (Saturated Fat 3g; Trans Fat 0g); Cholesterol 10mg; Sodium 60mg; Total Carbohydrate 16g (Dietary Fiber 0g; Sugars 10g); Protein 1g **% Daily Value:** Vitamin A 0%; Vitamin C 0%; Calcium 0%; Iron 6% **Exchanges:** ½ Starch, ½ Other Carbohydrate, 1 Fat **Carbohydrate Choices:** 1

choconut chippers

DEBORAH ANDERSON
Fairborn, OH
Bake-Off® Contest 32, 1986

6 DOZEN COOKIES

PREP TIME: *1 hour 25 minutes*
START TO FINISH: *1 hour 25 minutes*

¾ cup granulated sugar

¾ cup packed brown sugar

¼ cup vegetable oil

1 teaspoon vanilla

2 egg whites or 1 whole egg

1 box (6-serving size) chocolate fudge pudding and pie filling mix (not instant)

1 container (8 oz) sour cream (1 cup)

2 cups Pillsbury BEST® all-purpose flour

1½ cups quick-cooking or old-fashioned oats

1 teaspoon baking soda

½ teaspoon salt

2 cups chopped pecans

1 bag (12 oz) semisweet chocolate chips (2 cups)

1 Heat oven to 375°F. Grease cookie sheets with shortening or cooking spray. In large bowl, beat sugars, oil, vanilla, egg whites, pudding mix and sour cream with electric mixer on low speed until moistened; beat on medium speed 2 minutes, scraping bowl occasionally.

2 On low speed, beat in flour, oats, baking soda and salt until blended. Stir in pecans and chocolate chips. If necessary, cover with plastic wrap and refrigerate 1 hour for easier handling.

3 Onto cookie sheets, drop dough by rounded tablespoonfuls 2 inches apart.

4 Bake 6 to 7 minutes or until set. Cool 1 minute; remove from cookie sheets.

High Altitude (3500–6500 ft): No change.

1 Cookie: Calories 110 (Calories from Fat 45); Total Fat 5g (Saturated Fat 1.5g; Trans Fat 0g); Cholesterol 0mg; Sodium 50mg; Total Carbohydrate 13g (Dietary Fiber 0g; Sugars 8g); Protein 1g **% Daily Value:** Vitamin A 0%; Vitamin C 0%; Calcium 0%; Iron 2% **Exchanges:** 1 Other Carbohydrate, 1 Fat **Carbohydrate Choices:** 1

macaroonies

3 DOZEN COOKIES

PREP TIME: *1 hour 5 minutes*

START TO FINISH: *1 hour 5 minutes*

JUDITH ANN CARLSON
Amery, WI
Bake-Off® Contest 15, 1963

1 Heat oven to 325°F. Lightly grease cookie sheets with shortening or cooking spray; lightly flour.

2 In small bowl, beat eggs and salt with electric mixer on medium speed until foamy. Gradually add sugar, beating 5 to 7 minutes or until thick and ivory colored. With spoon, fold in flour and butter until well blended. Stir in remaining ingredients.

3 Onto cookie sheets, drop dough by rounded teaspoonfuls 2 inches apart.

4 Bake 12 to 15 minutes until delicately browned. Cool 1 minute; remove from cookie sheets.

High Altitude (3500–6500 ft): No change.

2 eggs

⅛ teaspoon salt

¾ cup sugar

½ cup Pillsbury BEST® all-purpose flour

1 tablespoon butter or margarine, melted

2 cups flaked coconut

1 cup semisweet chocolate chips (6 oz)

1 teaspoon grated lemon or orange peel

1 teaspoon vanilla

1 Cookie: Calories 80 (Calories from Fat 30); Total Fat 3.5g (Saturated Fat 2.5g; Trans Fat 0g); Cholesterol 15mg; Sodium 25mg; Total Carbohydrate 10g (Dietary Fiber 0g; Sugars 8g); Protein 0g **% Daily Value:** Vitamin A 0%; Vitamin C 0%; Calcium 0%; Iron 0% **Exchanges:** 1 Other Carbohydrate, ½ Fat **Carbohydrate Choices:** ½

molasses–oat bran cookies

CONSTANCE DUDLEY
Stanardsville, VA
Bake-Off® Contest 34, 1990

5 DOZEN COOKIES

PREP TIME: *1 hour 10 minutes*
START TO FINISH: *2 hours 10 minutes*

1 cup sugar

¾ cup vegetable oil

¼ cup fat-free egg product or 1 egg

¼ cup molasses

1½ cups Pillsbury BEST® whole wheat flour

1½ cups quick-cooking oats

½ cup oat bran

2 teaspoons baking soda

1 teaspoon ground cinnamon

½ teaspoon ground ginger

¼ teaspoon salt

¼ teaspoon ground cloves

¼ cup sugar

1 In large bowl, mix 1 cup sugar, the oil, egg product and molasses with electric mixer on medium speed until blended. On low speed, beat in flour, oats, oat bran, baking soda, cinnamon, ginger, salt and cloves until well blended. Cover with plastic wrap; refrigerate at least 1 hour for easier handling.

2 Heat oven to 375°F. Spray cookie sheets with cooking spray. Shape dough into 1-inch balls; roll in ¼ cup sugar. Place 2 inches apart on cookie sheets. With bottom of glass dipped in sugar, flatten balls slightly.

3 Bake 7 to 10 minutes or until cookies are set and tops are cracked. Cool 1 minute; remove from cookie sheets.

High Altitude (3500–6500 ft): Increase whole wheat flour to 1¾ cups.

1 Cookie: Calories 70 (Calories from Fat 25); Total Fat 3g (Saturated Fat 0g; Trans Fat 0g); Cholesterol 0mg; Sodium 55mg; Total Carbohydrate 9g (Dietary Fiber 0g; Sugars 5g); Protein 0g **% Daily Value:** Vitamin A 0%; Vitamin C 0%; Calcium 0%; Iron 0% **Exchanges:** ½ Starch, ½ Fat **Carbohydrate Choices:** ½

caramel–pecan sticky bun cookies

3 DOZEN COOKIES

PREP TIME: *1 hour*

START TO FINISH: *1 hour*

BETTY J. NICHOLS
Eugene, OR
Bake-Off® Contest 35, 1992

1 In large bowl, beat 1 cup butter and the granulated sugar with electric mixer on medium speed, scraping bowl occasionally, until light and fluffy. Beat in ½ cup corn syrup and the egg yolks. On low speed, beat in flour until well blended. If necessary, cover with plastic wrap and refrigerate 1 hour for easier handling.

2 In 1-quart saucepan, mix powdered sugar, ¼ cup butter and 3 tablespoons corn syrup; heat to boiling. Remove from heat. Stir in pecans. Refrigerate at least 10 minutes.

3 Meanwhile, heat oven to 375°F. Lightly grease cookie sheets with shortening or cooking spray. Shape dough into 1½-inch balls. Place 2 inches apart on cookie sheets.

4 Bake 5 minutes. Brush dough lightly with egg white. With spoon, carefully make deep indentation in center of each cookie; fill each with ½ teaspoon filling. Bake 6 to 9 minutes longer or until light golden brown. Cool 1 to 2 minutes; remove from cookie sheets.

High Altitude (3500–6500 ft): Decrease butter in cookies to ¾ cup; decrease dark corn syrup in cookies to ⅓ cup. Bake on ungreased cookie sheets.

COOKIES

1 cup butter or margarine, softened

½ cup granulated sugar

½ cup dark corn syrup

2 egg yolks

2½ cups Pillsbury BEST®
all-purpose flour

FILLING

½ cup powdered sugar

¼ cup butter or margarine

3 tablespoons dark corn syrup

½ cup coarsely chopped
pecans, toasted*

1 egg white, slightly beaten

*To toast pecans, bake uncovered in ungreased shallow pan in 350°F oven 6 to 10 minutes, stirring occasionally, until light brown. Or cook in ungreased heavy skillet over medium heat 5 to 7 minutes, stirring frequently until nuts begin to brown, then stirring constantly until light brown.

1 Cookie: Calories 140 (Calories from Fat 70); Total Fat 8g (Saturated Fat 4g; Trans Fat 0g); Cholesterol 30mg; Sodium 50mg; Total Carbohydrate 16g (Dietary Fiber 0g; Sugars 7g); Protein 1g **% Daily Value:** Vitamin A 4%; Vitamin C 0%; Calcium 0%; Iron 2% **Exchanges:** ½ Starch, ½ Other Carbohydrate, 1½ Fat **Carbohydrate Choices:** 1

apricot–almond squares

SANDY MUNSON

LaJunta, CO

Bake-Off® Contest 32, 1986

36 BARS

PREP TIME: *20 minutes*

START TO FINISH: *2 hours*

BASE

1 box (18.25 oz) Pillsbury® Moist
  Supreme® classic yellow or classic
  white cake mix

½ cup butter or margarine, melted

½ cup finely chopped almonds

1 cup apricot preserves

FILLING

1 package (8 oz) cream
  cheese, softened

¼ cup sugar

2 tablespoons Pillsbury BEST®
  all-purpose flour

⅛ teaspoon salt

1 teaspoon vanilla

1 egg

⅓ cup apricot preserves

½ cup coconut

1 Heat oven to 350°F (325°F for dark or nonstick pan). Generously grease bottom and sides of 13 × 9-inch pan with shortening or cooking spray. In large bowl, beat cake mix and butter with electric mixer on low speed until crumbly. Stir in almonds. Reserve 1 cup base mixture in small bowl. Press remaining mixture in bottom of pan.

2 Carefully spread 1 cup preserves over base (for easier spreading, preserves can be warmed slightly).

3 In the large bowl, beat cream cheese, sugar, flour, salt, vanilla and egg on low speed until well blended. Beat in ⅓ cup preserves. Carefully spread mixture over base. Stir coconut into reserved 1 cup base mixture; sprinkle over filling.

4 Bake 30 to 40 minutes or until golden brown and center is set. Cool completely, about 1 hour. For bars, cut into 6 rows by 6 rows. Store in refrigerator.

High Altitude (3500–6500 ft): No change.

1 Bar: Calories 160 (Calories from Fat 70); Total Fat 7g (Saturated Fat 4g; Trans Fat 0.5g); Cholesterol 20mg; Sodium 150mg; Total Carbohydrate 23g (Dietary Fiber 0g; Sugars 14g); Protein 2g **% Daily Value:** Vitamin A 4%; Vitamin C 0%; Calcium 4%; Iron 2% **Exchanges:** ½ Starch, 1 Other Carbohydrate, 1½ Fat **Carbohydrate Choices:** 1½

fudge–nut layer bars

24 BARS

PREP TIME: *30 minutes*

START TO FINISH: *2 hours*

MRS. J. TREJO
Chula Vista, CA
Bake-Off® Contest 14, 1962

1 Heat oven to 350°F. Grease 9-inch or 8-inch square pan with shortening or cooking spray. In 2-quart saucepan, heat chocolate chips, milk and 1 tablespoon butter over low heat, stirring constantly, until chocolate is melted; remove from heat. Stir in walnuts and 1 teaspoon vanilla.

2 In large bowl, mix all crust ingredients until coarse particles. Press half of mixture in pan. Spread filling carefully over crust. Sprinkle with remaining crust mixture.

3 Bake 25 to 30 minutes or until lightly browned. Cool about 1 hour. For bars, cut into 6 rows by 4 rows.

High Altitude (3500–6500 ft): Bake 30 to 35 minutes.

FILLING
- 1 cup semisweet chocolate chips (6 oz)
- ½ cup sweetened condensed milk (not evaporated)
- 1 tablespoon butter or margarine
- ½ cup chopped walnuts
- 1 teaspoon vanilla

CRUST
- 1½ cups quick-cooking oats
- 1¼ cups Pillsbury BEST® all-purpose flour
- 1 cup packed brown sugar
- ½ cup butter or margarine, softened
- 1 teaspoon vanilla
- ½ teaspoon baking soda
- ½ teaspoon salt
- 1 egg

1 Bar: Calories 200 (Calories from Fat 80); Total Fat 9g (Saturated Fat 4.5g; Trans Fat 0g); Cholesterol 20mg; Sodium 120mg; Total Carbohydrate 26g (Dietary Fiber 1g; Sugars 16g); Protein 3g **% Daily Value:** Vitamin A 4%; Vitamin C 0%; Calcium 4%; Iron 6% **Exchanges:** ½ Starch, 1 Other Carbohydrate, ½ High-Fat Meat, 1 Fat **Carbohydrate Choices:** 2

crispy date bars

MISS MARLA WILKINS
Tingley, IA
Bake-Off® Contest 28, 1978

24 BARS

PREP TIME: *30 minutes*
START TO FINISH: *2 hours*

CRUST
1 cup Pillsbury BEST® all-purpose flour
½ cup packed brown sugar
½ cup butter or margarine, softened

FILLING
1 cup chopped dates
½ cup granulated sugar
½ cup butter or margarine
1 egg
2 cups crisp rice cereal
1 cup chopped nuts
1 teaspoon vanilla

FROSTING
1 package (3 oz) cream cheese, softened
2 cups powdered sugar
½ teaspoon vanilla
1 tablespoon milk

1 Heat oven to 375°F. In small bowl, mix flour, brown sugar and ½ cup butter until crumbly. Press into ungreased 11 × 7-inch or 9-inch square pan. Bake 10 to 12 minutes or until golden brown.

2 Meanwhile, in 2-quart saucepan, cook dates, granulated sugar and ½ cup butter over medium heat, stirring constantly, until mixture boils. Simmer uncovered 3 minutes. In another small bowl, beat egg with fork until well blended. Stir about ¼ cup hot date mixture into beaten egg; return to saucepan. Cook, stirring constantly, until mixture boils. Remove from heat. Stir in cereal, nuts and 1 teaspoon vanilla.

3 Spread date mixture over baked crust. Cool 1 hour 30 minutes.

4 In medium bowl, beat all frosting ingredients with electric mixer on low speed until smooth. Spread over filling. For bars, cut into 6 rows by 4 rows. Store in refrigerator.

High Altitude (3500–6500 ft): Bake crust 12 to 14 minutes.

1 Bar: Calories 240 (Calories from Fat 110); Total Fat 12g (Saturated Fat 6g; Trans Fat 0g); Cholesterol 35mg; Sodium 70mg; Total Carbohydrate 30g (Dietary Fiber 1g; Sugars 23g); Protein 2g **% Daily Value:** Vitamin A 6%; Vitamin C 0%; Calcium 0%; Iron 6% **Exchanges:** ½ Starch, 1½ Other Carbohydrate, 2½ Fat **Carbohydrate Choices:** 2

nutty chocolate–pretzel bars

PATRICE HURD
Bemidji, MN
Bake-Off® Contest 40, 2002

36 BARS

PREP TIME: *20 minutes*
START TO FINISH: *1 hour 45 minutes*

1 can (10 oz) deluxe salted mixed nuts
(coarsely chop Brazil nuts)

1 roll (16.5 oz) Pillsbury® Create 'n
Bake® refrigerated sugar cookies

1 cup toffee bits

1½ cups milk chocolate chips (9 oz)

⅓ cup butterscotch chips

⅓ cup creamy peanut butter

1 cup coarsely chopped salted pretzels

1 oz vanilla-flavored candy coating
(almond bark), chopped, or
2 tablespoons white vanilla
baking chips

1 Heat oven to 375°F. Spray 13 × 9-inch pan with cooking spray. In bottom of pan, spread nuts. Cut cookie dough into ½-inch slices; place over nuts in pan. With floured fingers, press evenly to form crust. Sprinkle toffee bits over crust; press in lightly.

2 Bake 20 to 25 minutes or until golden brown. Cool 30 minutes.

3 In large microwavable bowl, place chocolate chips and butterscotch chips. Microwave on High 1 minute 30 seconds to 2 minutes, stirring every 30 seconds, until melted and smooth. Stir in peanut butter until well blended. Fold in pretzels. Spread mixture evenly over baked crust.

4 In small microwavable bowl, place candy coating. Microwave on High 30 to 60 seconds, stirring every 15 seconds, until melted and smooth. Drizzle over bars. Refrigerate until chocolate is set, about 30 minutes. For bars, cut into 6 rows by 6 rows.

High Altitude (3500–6500 ft): No change.

1 Bar: Calories 230 (Calories from Fat 130); Total Fat 14g (Saturated Fat 5g; Trans Fat 1g); Cholesterol 15mg; Sodium 110mg; Total Carbohydrate 23g (Dietary Fiber 0g; Sugars 17g); Protein 3g **% Daily Value:** Vitamin A 2%; Vitamin C 0%; Calcium 2%; Iron 4% **Exchanges:** 1½ Other Carbohydrate, ½ High-Fat Meat, 2 Fat **Carbohydrate Choices:** 1½

chocolate chip–popcorn bars

36 BARS

PREP TIME: *20 minutes*
START TO FINISH: *2 hours 10 minutes*

FRAN NEAVOLL
Salem, OR
Bake-Off® Contest 41, 2004

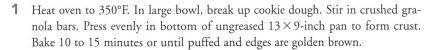

1 Heat oven to 350°F. In large bowl, break up cookie dough. Stir in crushed granola bars. Press evenly in bottom of ungreased 13 × 9-inch pan to form crust. Bake 10 to 15 minutes or until puffed and edges are golden brown.

2 Remove from oven. Immediately sprinkle with marshmallows. Return to oven; bake 1 to 2 minutes longer or until marshmallows begin to puff.

3 In 3-quart saucepan, heat corn syrup, butter and peanut butter chips over medium heat 3 to 4 minutes, stirring frequently, until chips are melted and mixture is smooth. Stir in popcorn (mixture will be thick). Spoon over marshmallows; spread evenly to just barely cover marshmallows. Cool 30 minutes.

4 In small microwavable bowl, microwave chocolate chips on High 1 minute to 1 minute 30 seconds, stirring once after about 30 seconds, until melted. Pour melted chocolate into quart-size resealable food-storage plastic bag. Cut off tiny bottom corner of bag; drizzle chocolate over bars. Refrigerate at least 1 hour before serving. For bars, cut into 6 rows by 6 rows.

High Altitude (3500–6500 ft): In step 1, bake crust 13 to 18 minutes.

CRUST

1 roll (16.5 oz) Pillsbury® Create 'n Bake™ refrigerated chocolate chip cookies

4 oats 'n honey crunchy granola bars (2 pouches from 8.9-oz box), crushed*

TOPPING

3½ cups miniature marshmallows

⅔ cup light corn syrup

¼ cup butter or margarine

1 bag (10 oz) peanut butter chips (1⅔ cups)

1 bag (3.5 oz) butter flavor microwave popcorn, popped

1 cup semisweet chocolate chips (6 oz)

1 Bar: Calories 190 (Calories from Fat 80); Total Fat 9g (Saturated Fat 3g; Trans Fat 1g); Cholesterol 5mg; Sodium 110mg; Total Carbohydrate 27g (Dietary Fiber 0g; Sugars 17g); Protein 2g **% Daily Value:** Vitamin A 0%; Vitamin C 0%; Calcium 0%; Iron 2% **Exchanges:** ½ Starch, 1 Other Carbohydrate, 2 Fat **Carbohydrate Choices:** 2

*To easily crush granola bars, do not unwrap. Use rolling pin to crush bars.

caramel-cashew bars

KATHLEEN KILDSIG
Kiel, WI
Bake-Off® Contest 40, 2002

36 BARS

PREP TIME: *20 minutes*
START TO FINISH: *1 hour 25 minutes*

1 roll (16.5 oz) Pillsbury® Create 'n Bake™ refrigerated chocolate chip cookies

1 bag (11.5 oz) milk chocolate chips (2 cups)

1 container (16 oz) caramel apple dip (1½ cups)

3 cups crisp rice cereal

1¼ cups chopped cashews

1 Heat oven to 375°F. Cut cookie dough in half crosswise. Cut each section in half lengthwise. Press dough in bottom of ungreased 13 × 9-inch pan.

2 Bake 10 to 18 minutes or until light golden brown. Cool 15 minutes.

3 In 3-quart saucepan, cook 1 cup of the chocolate chips and 1 cup of the dip over medium heat, stirring constantly, until melted and smooth. Remove from heat. Stir in cereal and cashews. Spread over cooled crust.

4 In 1-quart saucepan, cook remaining 1 cup chocolate chips and ½ cup dip over medium heat, stirring constantly, until melted and smooth. Spread over cereal mixture. Refrigerate about 30 minutes or until set. For bars, cut into 6 rows by 6 rows.

High Altitude (3500–6500 ft): No change.

1 Bar: Calories 170 (Calories from Fat 60); Total Fat 7g (Saturated Fat 2.5g; Trans Fat 0g); Cholesterol 0mg; Sodium 90mg; Total Carbohydrate 24g (Dietary Fiber 0g; Sugars 17g); Protein 2g **% Daily Value:** Vitamin A 0%; Vitamin C 0%; Calcium 2%; Iron 6% **Exchanges:** ½ Starch, 1 Other Carbohydrate, 1½ Fat **Carbohydrate Choices:** 1½

chocodiles

48 BARS

PREP TIME: *25 minutes*

START TO FINISH: *2 hours 45 minutes*

ELIZABETH WICKERSHAM
Fort Lauderdale, FL
Bake-Off® Contest 09, 1957

1   Heat oven to 350°F. In large bowl, beat brown sugar, butter, shortening, ⅓ cup peanut butter and the vanilla with electric mixer on low speed until light and fluffy. Add egg; beating well. Add flour and salt; beat until dough forms.

2   Using metal spatula, spread mixture evenly in bottom of ungreased 15 × 10 × 1-inch pan.

3   Bake 20 to 25 minutes or until light golden brown. Cool slightly. Meanwhile, in 2-quart saucepan, melt chocolate chips and ¾ cup peanut butter over low heat, stirring constantly. Stir in cereal.

4   Spread chocolate mixture over baked layer. Let stand at room temperature about 2 hours until chocolate hardens. For bars, cut into 8 rows by 6 rows.

High Altitude (3500–6500 ft): No change.

BASE
1¼ cups packed brown sugar

½ cup butter or margarine, softened

½ cup shortening

⅓ cup crunchy peanut butter

1 teaspoon vanilla

1 egg

2½ cups Pillsbury BEST®
all-purpose flour

¼ teaspoon salt

CHOCOLATE CRUNCH
1½ cups semisweet chocolate
chips (9 oz)

¾ cup crunchy peanut butter

1½ cups slightly crushed corn
flakes cereal

1 Bar: Calories 160 (Calories from Fat 80); Total Fat 9g (Saturated Fat 3.5g; Trans Fat 0g); Cholesterol 10mg; Sodium 65mg; Total Carbohydrate 16g (Dietary Fiber 0g; Sugars 9g); Protein 3g **% Daily Value:** Vitamin A 0%; Vitamin C 0%; Calcium 0%; Iron 6% **Exchanges:** ½ Starch, ½ Other Carbohydrate, 2 Fat **Carbohydrate Choices:** 1

chocolate chip, oats 'n' caramel cookie squares

NIELA FRANTELLIZZI
Boca Raton, FL
Bake-Off® Contest 37, 1996

16 SQUARES
PREP TIME: *35 minutes*
START TO FINISH: *2 hours 40 minutes*

1 roll (16.5 oz) Pillsbury® Create 'n Bake™ refrigerated chocolate chip cookies

1 cup quick-cooking oats

Dash salt, if desired

⅔ cup caramel topping

5 tablespoons Pillsbury BEST® all-purpose flour

1 teaspoon vanilla

¾ cup chopped walnuts

1 cup semisweet chocolate chips (6 oz)

1 Heat oven to 350°F. In large bowl, break up cookie dough. Stir or knead in oats and salt. Reserve ½ cup dough for topping. In ungreased 9-inch square pan, press remaining dough mixture evenly in bottom to form crust.

2 Bake 10 to 12 minutes or until dough puffs and appears dry.

3 In small bowl, mix caramel topping, flour and vanilla until well blended. Sprinkle walnuts and chocolate chips evenly over crust. Drizzle evenly with caramel mixture. Crumble reserved ½ cup dough mixture over caramel.

4 Bake 20 to 25 minutes longer or until golden brown. Cool 10 minutes. Run knife around sides of pan to loosen bars. Cool completely, about 1 hour 30 minutes. For squares, cut into 4 rows by 4 rows. Store tightly covered.

High Altitude (3500–6500 ft): In step 2, bake crust 12 to 14 minutes. In step 4, bake 22 to 27 minutes.

1 Bar: Calories 280 (Calories from Fat 110); Total Fat 12g (Saturated Fat 4g; Trans Fat 1g); Cholesterol 5mg; Sodium 140mg; Total Carbohydrate 40g (Dietary Fiber 1g; Sugars 24g); Protein 4g **% Daily Value:** Vitamin A 0%; Vitamin C 0%; Calcium 0%; Iron 6% **Exchanges:** 1 Starch, 1½ Other Carbohydrate, 2½ Fat **Carbohydrate Choices:** 2½

walnut fudge bars

MABEL PATENT
Kelseyville, CA
Bake-Off® Contest 39, 2000

36 BARS
PREP TIME: *15 minutes*
START TO FINISH: *4 hours 20 minutes*

1 box (19.5 oz) Pillsbury® fudge
  brownie mix

½ cup butter or margarine, melted

¼ cup water

2 eggs

2 cups quick-cooking oats

2 cups chopped walnuts

1 bag (12 oz) semisweet chocolate
  chips (2 cups)

1 can (14 oz) sweetened condensed
  milk (not evaporated)

1   Heat oven to 350°F. Grease 13 × 9-inch pan with shortening or cooking spray. In large bowl, mix brownie mix, butter, water and eggs; beat 50 strokes with spoon. Stir in oats and walnuts.

2   In medium microwavable bowl, mix chocolate chips and milk. Microwave uncovered on High 1 minute 30 seconds, stirring twice, until chips are melted and mixture is smooth.

3   Spread half of brownie batter in pan. Spread chocolate mixture over batter. Drop remaining brownie batter by teaspoonfuls over chocolate layer. (Brownie mixture will not completely cover chocolate layer.)

4   Bake 29 to 33 minutes or until brownie topping feels dry and edges begin to pull away from sides of pan. DO NOT OVERBAKE. Cool at room temperature 2 hours. Refrigerate 1 hour 30 minutes. For bars, cut into 6 rows by 6 rows. Serve cold or at room temperature. Store in refrigerator.

High Altitude (3500–6500 ft): Add ⅓ cup all-purpose flour to dry brownie mix.

1 Bar: Calories 240 (Calories from Fat 110); Total Fat 13g (Saturated Fat 4.5g; Trans Fat 0g); Cholesterol 20mg; Sodium 80mg; Total Carbohydrate 29g (Dietary Fiber 2g; Sugars 20g); Protein 4g **% Daily Value:** Vitamin A 2%; Vitamin C 0%; Calcium 4%; Iron 8% **Exchanges:** ½ Starch, 1½ Other Carbohydrate, 2½ Fat **Carbohydrate Choices:** 2

whole wheat–applesauce bars

24 BARS

PREP TIME: *25 minutes*
START TO FINISH: *1 hour 50 minutes*

JANELLE SMITH
Bunker Hill, WV
Bake-Off® Contest 30, 1982

1 Heat oven to 350°F. Grease 13 × 9-inch pan with shortening or cooking spray. In small bowl, stir together flours, baking powder, baking soda, salt and cinnamon; set aside.

2 In large bowl, beat granulated sugar, brown sugar, ½ cup butter and the molasses with electric mixer on medium speed until light and fluffy. Beat in egg. Beat in applesauce and sour cream. On low speed, gradually beat in flour mixture until well blended. Stir in ½ cup walnuts. Spread in pan.

3 Bake 20 to 25 minutes or until toothpick inserted in center comes out clean. Cool completely, about 1 hour.

4 In small bowl, beat all frosting ingredients except ¼ cup walnuts on medium speed until smooth and creamy. Spread frosting over bars. Sprinkle with walnuts. For bars, cut into 6 rows by 4 rows. Store in refrigerator.

High Altitude (3500–6500 ft): No change.

BARS
¾ cup Pillsbury BEST® all-purpose flour
¾ cup Pillsbury BEST® whole wheat flour
1 teaspoon baking powder
¼ teaspoon baking soda
¼ teaspoon salt
¼ teaspoon ground cinnamon
½ cup granulated sugar
¼ cup packed brown sugar
½ cup butter or margarine, softened
¼ cup molasses
1 egg
½ cup applesauce
¼ cup sour cream
½ cup chopped walnuts

FROSTING
1 cup powdered sugar
2 tablespoons butter or margarine, softened
1½ oz cream cheese (from 3-oz package), softened
1½ teaspoons milk
½ teaspoon vanilla
¼ cup finely chopped walnuts

1 Bar: Calories 170 (Calories from Fat 80); Total Fat 9g (Saturated Fat 4g; Trans Fat 0g); Cholesterol 25mg; Sodium 105mg; Total Carbohydrate 22g (Dietary Fiber 0g; Sugars 14g); Protein 2g **% Daily Value:** Vitamin A 4%; Vitamin C 0%; Calcium 4%; Iron 4% **Exchanges:** ½ Starch, 1 Other Carbohydrate, 1½ Fat **Carbohydrate Choices:** 1½

tropical pineapple-coconut bars

MAUREEN PINEGAR
Midvale, UT
Bake-Off® Contest 35, 1992

36 BARS
PREP TIME: *30 minutes*
START TO FINISH: *2 hours 10 minutes*

BASE

1 box (18.25 oz) Pillsbury® Moist
    Supreme® classic yellow cake mix
1½ cups quick-cooking oats
½ cup butter or margarine, softened
1 egg

FILLING

½ cup Pillsbury BEST® all-purpose flour
1 can (14 oz) sweetened condensed
    milk (not evaporated)
1 can (8 oz) crushed pineapple, well
    drained, liquid reserved for Glaze
½ teaspoon ground nutmeg

TOPPING

1 cup chopped macadamia nuts
1 cup coconut
1 cup white vanilla baking chips (6 oz)

GLAZE

1 cup powdered sugar
4 to 6 teaspoons reserved
    pineapple liquid

1 Heat oven to 350°F. Lightly grease 13 × 9-inch pan with shortening or cooking spray. In large bowl, beat all base ingredients with electric mixer on low speed until crumbly. Reserve 1½ cups of the crumb mixture in medium bowl. Press remaining crumb mixture in bottom of pan.

2 In another medium bowl, stir together all filling ingredients; pour over crust in pan. To reserved 1½ cups crumb mixture, add all topping ingredients; mix well. Sprinkle topping mixture evenly over filling.

3 Bake 30 to 40 minutes or until golden brown. Cool completely, about 1 hour.

4 In small bowl, stir together powdered sugar and enough reserved pineapple liquid until smooth and thin enough to drizzle. Drizzle glaze over bars. For bars, cut into 6 rows by 6 rows. Store in refrigerator.

High Altitude (3500–6500 ft): No change.

1 Bar: Calories 230 (Calories from Fat 90); Total Fat 10g (Saturated Fat 5g; Trans Fat 0g); Cholesterol 15mg; Sodium 150mg; Total Carbohydrate 31g (Dietary Fiber 0g; Sugars 24g); Protein 3g **% Daily Value:** Vitamin A 2%; Vitamin C 0%; Calcium 6%; Iron 4% **Exchanges:** 1 Starch, 1 Other Carbohydrate, 2 Fat **Carbohydrate Choices:** 2

chewy chocolate–peanut butter bars

MARJORIE BERGEMANN
Greenbelt, MD
Bake-Off® Contest 39, 2000

36 BARS
PREP TIME: *15 minutes*
START TO FINISH: *2 hours 45 minutes*

1 roll (16.5 oz) Pillsbury® Create 'n Bake™ refrigerated sugar cookies

1 can (14 oz) sweetened condensed milk (not evaporated)

1 cup crunchy peanut butter

1 teaspoon vanilla

3 egg yolks

1 bag (12 oz) semisweet chocolate chips (2 cups)

1 Heat oven to 350°F. Spray 13 × 9-inch pan with cooking spray. Cut cookie dough in half crosswise. Cut each section in half lengthwise. With floured fingers, press dough evenly in bottom of pan to form crust. Bake 10 minutes.

2 Meanwhile, in medium bowl, mix milk, peanut butter, vanilla and egg yolks until smooth.

3 Spoon milk mixture evenly over partially baked crust; carefully spread. Bake 20 to 25 minutes longer or until set.

4 Sprinkle with chocolate chips; let stand 3 minutes to soften. Spread chocolate evenly over top. Cool completely, about 1 hour 30 minutes. Refrigerate until chocolate is set, about 30 minutes. For bars, cut into 6 rows by 6 rows.

High Altitude (3500–6500 ft): In step 1, bake crust 12 to 15 minutes.

1 Bar: Calories 190 (Calories from Fat 90); Total Fat 10g (Saturated Fat 4g; Trans Fat 0.5g); Cholesterol 25mg; Sodium 85mg; Total Carbohydrate 21g (Dietary Fiber 0g; Sugars 16g); Protein 4g **% Daily Value:** Vitamin A 0%; Vitamin C 0%; Calcium 4%; Iron 4% **Exchanges:** ½ Starch, 1 Other Carbohydrate, 2 Fat **Carbohydrate Choices:** 1½

white chocolate–key lime calypso bars

DIDI FRAIOLI
Huntington, NY
Bake-Off® Contest 40, 2002

36 BARS
PREP TIME: *20 minutes*
START TO FINISH: *3 hours 5 minutes*

1 roll (16.5 oz) Pillsbury® Create 'n Bake™ refrigerated sugar cookies

1 cup chopped pistachio nuts

1 cup coconut

1½ cups white vanilla baking chips (9 oz)

1 can (14 oz) sweetened condensed milk (not evaporated)

½ cup Key lime juice, fresh lime juice or frozen (thawed) limeade concentrate

3 egg yolks

1 teaspoon vegetable oil

1 Heat oven to 350°F. Grease 13 × 9-inch pan with shortening or cooking spray. In large bowl, break up cookie dough. Stir or knead in nuts and coconut until well blended. With floured fingers, press dough mixture evenly in bottom of pan to form crust. Sprinkle 1 cup of the vanilla baking chips over dough; press lightly into dough.

2 Bake 14 to 16 minutes or until light golden brown. Meanwhile, in medium bowl, beat condensed milk, lime juice and egg yolks with spoon until well blended.

3 Remove crust from oven. Pour milk mixture evenly over crust. Bake 20 to 25 minutes longer or until filling is set.

4 In small microwavable bowl, place remaining ½ cup vanilla baking chips and the oil. Microwave uncovered on High 45 seconds. Stir until smooth; if necessary, microwave an additional 15 seconds. Drizzle over warm bars. Cool at room temperature 1 hour. Refrigerate until chilled, about 1 hour. For bars, cut into 6 rows by 6 rows. Store in refrigerator.

High Altitude (3500–6500 ft): In step 2, bake crust 16 to 18 minutes.

1 Bar: Calories 190 (Calories from Fat 90); Total Fat 10g (Saturated Fat 4.5g; Trans Fat 0.5g); Cholesterol 25mg; Sodium 65mg; Total Carbohydrate 23g (Dietary Fiber 0g; Sugars 18g); Protein 3g **% Daily Value:** Vitamin A 0%; Vitamin C 0%; Calcium 6%; Iron 2% **Exchanges:** ½ Starch, 1 Other Carbohydrate, 2 Fat **Carbohydrate Choices:** 1½

choco-nut sweet treats

AGATHA L. ROTH
Indianapolis, IN
Bake-Off® Contest 37, 1996

48 BARS
PREP TIME: *20 minutes*
START TO FINISH: *2 hours 20 minutes*

CRUST
1 roll (16.5 oz) Pillsbury® Create 'n Bake™ refrigerated chocolate chip cookies, well chilled

FILLING
2 eggs

2 teaspoons vanilla

1 container (15 oz) Pillsbury® Creamy Supreme® coconut pecan frosting

1 can (14 oz) sweetened condensed milk (not evaporated)

TOPPING
1½ cups semisweet chocolate chips (9 oz)

3 tablespoons vegetable oil

1 cup coarsely chopped pecans or walnuts

1 Heat oven to 350°F. Cut cookie dough into ½-inch slices. In bottom of ungreased 15 × 10 × 1-inch pan, arrange dough slices. Using floured fingers, press dough evenly in pan to form crust. Bake 8 to 12 minutes or until light golden brown. Cool 5 minutes.

2 Meanwhile, in large bowl, beat eggs with electric mixer on medium speed until foamy. Add remaining filling ingredients; beat on medium speed about 1 minute or until well blended. Spoon and spread filling evenly over partially baked crust.

3 Bake 20 to 25 minutes longer or until top is deep golden brown and center is set. Cool 5 minutes.

4 In 1-quart saucepan, heat chocolate chips and oil over medium heat, stirring constantly, until chips are melted. Carefully pour over filling; gently spread to cover. Sprinkle with pecans. Refrigerate about 1 hour 30 minutes or until chocolate is set. For bars, cut into 8 rows by 6 rows. Store in refrigerator.

High Altitude (3500–6500 ft): In step 1, bake crust 12 to 16 minutes. Add ¼ cup all-purpose flour to filling. In step 3, bake 25 to 30 minutes.

1 Bar: Calories 160 (Calories from Fat 80); Total Fat 8g (Saturated Fat 3g; Trans Fat 0.5g); Cholesterol 15mg; Sodium 55mg; Total Carbohydrate 19g (Dietary Fiber 0g; Sugars 15g); Protein 2g **% Daily Value:** Vitamin A 0%; Vitamin C 0%; Calcium 2%; Iron 2% **Exchanges:** 1½ Other Carbohydrate, 1½ Fat **Carbohydrate Choices:** 1

Caramel Cream Sandwich Cookies (page 81) ▸

brownie macaroons

RONALD GRASGREEN
Sugarland, TX
Bake-Off® Contest 39, 2000

2 DOZEN COOKIES

PREP TIME: *45 minutes*
START TO FINISH: *45 minutes*

1 box (15.5 oz) Pillsbury® chocolate
  chunk brownie mix
2 cups coconut
2 tablespoons water
1 tablespoon vegetable oil
1 egg

1 Heat oven to 350°F. Lightly grease cookie sheets with shortening or cooking spray, or line with parchment paper. In large bowl, mix brownie mix and coconut. Stir in water, oil and egg until moistened.

2 Shape dough into 1½-inch balls. Place 3 inches apart on cookie sheet; flatten balls slightly.

3 Bake 12 to 15 minutes or until edges are set (centers will be soft).

High Altitude (3500–6500 ft): No change.

1 **Cookie:** Calories 120 (Calories from Fat 45); Total Fat 5g (Saturated Fat 3g; Trans Fat 0g); Cholesterol 10mg; Sodium 65mg; Total Carbohydrate 18g (Dietary Fiber 0g; Sugars 13g); Protein 1g **% Daily Value:** Vitamin A 0%; Vitamin C 0%; Calcium 0%; Iron 4% **Exchanges:** ½ Starch, ½ Other Carbohydrate, 1 Fat **Carbohydrate Choices:** 1

brazilian jubilee cookies

ABOUT 3 DOZEN COOKIES
PREP TIME: *1 hour 15 minutes*
START TO FINISH: *1 hour 15 minutes*

MRS. F.H. SPEERS
Midland, TX
Bake-Off® Contest 04, 1952

1 Heat oven to 350°F. Grease cookie sheets with shortening or cooking spray. In large bowl, beat sugars and shortening with electric mixer on medium speed, scraping bowl occasionally, until well blended. Beat in vanilla and egg. On low speed, beat in flour, instant coffee, baking powder, salt, cinnamon and 1 cup nuts until dough forms.

2 Shape dough by tablespoonfuls into balls. Place 2 inches apart on cookie sheets.

3 Bake 12 to 15 minutes or until golden brown. Immediately top each cookie with 1 chocolate star. Remove from cookie sheets; cool 5 minutes (chocolate will soften). Spread chocolate over cookies to frost. Sprinkle with additional chopped nuts.

High Altitude (3500–6500 ft): No change.

¾ cup granulated sugar

¼ cup packed brown sugar

½ cup shortening

2 teaspoons vanilla

1 egg

1½ cups Pillsbury BEST®
all-purpose flour

1 to 2 tablespoons instant coffee
granules or crystals

1 teaspoon baking powder

½ teaspoon salt

½ teaspoon ground cinnamon

1 cup chopped Brazil nuts

36 milk chocolate stars (from 14-oz bag)

Additional chopped Brazil nuts,
if desired

1 Cookie: Calories 120 (Calories from Fat 60); Total Fat 7g (Saturated Fat 2g; Trans Fat 0g); Cholesterol 5mg; Sodium 50mg; Total Carbohydrate 13g (Dietary Fiber 0g; Sugars 8g); Protein 2g **% Daily Value:** Vitamin A 0%; Vitamin C 0%; Calcium 2%; Iron 2% **Exchanges:** 1 Other Carbohydrate, 1½ Fat **Carbohydrate Choices:** 1

texan-sized almond crunch cookies

MRS. BARBARA HODGSON
Elkhart, IN
Bake-Off® Contest 30, 1982

4 DOZEN LARGE COOKIES
PREP TIME: *1 hour 55 minutes*
START TO FINISH: *1 hour 55 minutes*

1 cup granulated sugar

1 cup powdered sugar

1 cup butter or margarine, softened

1 cup vegetable oil

1 teaspoon almond extract

2 eggs

3½ cups Pillsbury BEST®
   all-purpose flour

1 cup Pillsbury BEST® whole
   wheat flour

1 teaspoon baking soda

1 teaspoon salt

1 teaspoon cream of tartar

2 cups coarsely chopped almonds

1¼ cups toffee bits (from 10-oz bag)

Additional granulated sugar
   (about ¼ cup)

1 Heat oven to 350°F. In large bowl, beat sugars, butter and oil with electric mixer on medium speed, scraping bowl occasionally, until well blended. Beat in almond extract and eggs. On low speed, gradually beat in flours, baking soda, salt and cream of tartar. Stir in almonds and toffee bits. If necessary, cover with plastic wrap and refrigerate 1 hour for easier handling.

2 Shape large tablespoonfuls of dough into balls; roll in additional granulated sugar. Place 5 inches apart on ungreased cookie sheets. With fork dipped in sugar, flatten balls in crisscross pattern.

3 Bake 12 to 18 minutes or until light golden brown around edges. Cool 1 minute; remove from cookie sheets.

High Altitude (3500–6500 ft): No change.

1 Large Cookie: Calories 210 (Calories from Fat 120); Total Fat 13g (Saturated Fat 4g; Trans Fat 0g); Cholesterol 20mg; Sodium 125mg; Total Carbohydrate 20g (Dietary Fiber 1g; Sugars 11g); Protein 3g **% Daily Value:** Vitamin A 2%; Vitamin C 0%; Calcium 0%; Iron 4% **Exchanges:** ½ Starch, 1 Other Carbohydrate, 2½ Fat **Carbohydrate Choices:** 1

peanut brittle cookies

MRS. JOHN HAMLON
Fergus Falls, MN
Bake-Off® Contest 04, 1952

2 DOZEN COOKIES

PREP TIME: *25 minutes*
START TO FINISH: *1 hour 20 minutes*

½ cup packed brown sugar

½ cup butter or margarine, softened

1 egg, beaten, 1 tablespoon reserved

1 teaspoon vanilla

1 cup Pillsbury BEST® all-purpose flour

¼ teaspoon baking soda

½ teaspoon ground cinnamon

½ cup salted peanuts, finely chopped

Reserved 1 tablespoon beaten egg

½ cup salted peanuts or other nuts

1 Heat oven to 325°F. Grease large cookie sheet with shortening or cooking spray. In large bowl, beat brown sugar and butter with electric mixer on medium speed, scraping bowl occasionally, until well blended. Beat in 2 tablespoons beaten egg and the vanilla. On low speed, beat in flour, baking soda and cinnamon until dough forms. Stir in ½ cup finely chopped peanuts. Refrigerate dough 30 minutes.

2 Crumble chilled dough onto cookie sheet. With floured hands, press dough into 14 × 10-inch rectangle. Brush with reserved 1 tablespoon egg. Sprinkle with ½ cup peanuts; press into dough.

3 Bake 20 to 25 minutes or until dark golden brown. Cool 5 minutes; while warm, cut or break into 24 pieces.

High Altitude (3500–6500 ft): Bake 20 to 23 minutes.

1 Cookie: Calories 110 (Calories from Fat 70); Total Fat 7g (Saturated Fat 3g; Trans Fat 0g); Cholesterol 20mg; Sodium 65mg; Total Carbohydrate 9g (Dietary Fiber 0g; Sugars 5g); Protein 3g **% Daily Value:** Vitamin A 2%; Vitamin C 0%; Calcium 0%; Iron 2% **Exchanges:** ½ Other Carbohydrate, ½ High-Fat Meat, ½ Fat **Carbohydrate Choices:** ½

easy-bake butterscotch crispies

48 BARS

PREP TIME: *20 minutes*
START TO FINISH: *1 hour 5 minutes*

MRS. RICHARD J. HUBER
Evans City, PA
Bake-Off® Contest 25, 1974

1 Heat oven to 325°F. In large bowl, beat butter, sugar and vanilla with electric mixer on medium speed, scraping bowl occasionally, until light and fluffy. With spoon, stir in flour, pudding mix, baking powder and nuts. Press evenly in ungreased 15 × 10 × 1-inch pan.

2 Bake 10 to 15 minutes or until edges are lightly browned. Immediately cut into 8 rows by 6 rows. Cool completely in pan on cooling rack, about 30 minutes.

High Altitude (3500–6500 ft): Bake 15 to 20 minutes.

1 cup butter or margarine, softened
½ cup sugar
1 teaspoon vanilla
2 cups Pillsbury BEST® all-purpose flour
1 box (4-serving size) butterscotch pudding and pie filling mix
1 teaspoon baking powder
½ cup chopped nuts

1 Cookie: Calories 80 (Calories from Fat 40); Total Fat 4.5g (Saturated Fat 2.5g; Trans Fat 0g); Cholesterol 10mg; Sodium 50mg; Total Carbohydrate 8g (Dietary Fiber 0g; Sugars 4g); Protein 0g **% Daily Value:** Vitamin A 2%; Vitamin C 0%; Calcium 0%; Iron 0% **Exchanges:** ½ Other Carbohydrate, 1 Fat **Carbohydrate Choices:** ½

hoot owl cookies

NATALIE R. RIGGIN
Olympia, WA
Bake-Off® Contest 08, 1956

40 COOKIES

PREP TIME: *1 hour*
START TO FINISH: *2 hours*

COOKIES

1 cup packed brown sugar
¾ cup butter or margarine, softened
1 teaspoon vanilla
1 egg
2¼ cups Pillsbury BEST®
   all-purpose flour
2 teaspoons baking powder
½ teaspoon salt
1½ oz unsweetened baking
   chocolate, melted
¼ teaspoon baking soda

GARNISH

80 semisweet chocolate chips
   (about ⅓ cup)
40 whole cashews (about ⅔ cup)

1 In large bowl, beat brown sugar and butter with electric mixer on medium speed 1 to 2 minutes, scraping bowl occasionally, until light and fluffy. Beat in vanilla and egg. On low speed, beat in flour, baking powder and salt until dough forms. In small bowl, place 1 cup of the dough; stir in melted chocolate and baking soda until well blended.

2 On 12 × 8-inch sheet of plastic wrap, press half of light dough to form 10 × 4-inch strip. Shape half of chocolate dough into roll 10 inches long; place on strip of light dough. Mold sides of light dough around chocolate dough; wrap in plastic wrap. Repeat with remaining dough. Refrigerate 1 hour for easier handling.

3 Heat oven to 350°F. Cut each roll into 40 (⅛ - to ¼-inch) slices; place 2 slices, sides touching, on ungreased cookie sheets to resemble owl faces. Pinch corner of each slice to form ears. Place chocolate chip in center of each slice for eyes; press whole cashew between slices for beak.

4 Bake 8 to 10 minutes or until edges are light golden brown. Immediately remove from cookie sheets.

High Altitude (3500–6500 ft): Decrease brown sugar to ¾ cup; increase all-purpose flour to 2½ cups.

1 Cookie: Calories 110 (Calories from Fat 60); Total Fat 7g (Saturated Fat 3.5g; Trans Fat 0g); Cholesterol 15mg; Sodium 170mg; Total Carbohydrate 12g (Dietary Fiber 0g; Sugars 7g); Protein 1g **% Daily Value:** Vitamin A 2%; Vitamin C 0%; Calcium 2%; Iron 4% **Exchanges:** ½ Starch, 1½ Fat **Carbohydrate Choices:** 1

choco–peanut butter cups

RONNA FARLEY
Rockville, MD
Bake-Off® Contest 42, 2006

24 COOKIE CUPS

PREP TIME: *40 minutes*
START TO FINISH: *1 hour 40 minutes*

1 roll (16.5 oz) Pillsbury® Create 'n Bake™ refrigerated peanut butter cookies

1 cup white vanilla baking chips (6 oz)

¾ cup creamy peanut butter

1 cup semisweet chocolate chips (6 oz)

¾ cup creamy peanut butter

4 oats 'n honey crunchy granola bars (2 pouches from 8.9-oz box), crushed (¾ cup)*

1 Heat oven to 350°F. Grease 24 mini muffin cups with cooking spray or shortening. Cut cookie dough into 24 slices. With floured fingers, press 1 slice in bottom and up side of each mini muffin cup, forming ¼-inch rim above top of cup.

2 Bake 10 to 15 minutes or until edges are deep golden brown. Cool in pans on cooling racks 5 minutes. With tip of handle of wooden spoon, press dough down in center of each cup to make room for 2 tablespoons filling.

3 Meanwhile, in 2-quart saucepan, melt vanilla baking chips and ¾ cup peanut butter over low heat, stirring constantly. Divide mixture evenly into cookie cups (about 1 tablespoon each). Refrigerate 10 minutes.

4 In same 2-quart saucepan, melt chocolate chips and ¾ cup peanut butter over low heat, stirring constantly. Divide chocolate mixture evenly on top of peanut butter mixture in each cup (about 1 tablespoon each). Sprinkle crushed granola bars over top of each. Refrigerate until set, about 1 hour. Remove from muffin cups before serving.

High Altitude (3500–6500 ft): Break up cookie dough into bowl; knead or stir ¼ cup all-purpose flour into dough. Divide dough into 24 pieces; press 1 piece in each cup.

*To easily crush granola bars, do not unwrap; use rolling pin to crush bars.

1 Cookie Cup: Calories 290 (Calories from Fat 160); Total Fat 17g (Saturated Fat 6g; Trans Fat 0.5g); Cholesterol 0mg; Sodium 200mg; Total Carbohydrate 27g (Dietary Fiber 1g; Sugars 18g); Protein 7g **% Daily Value:** Vitamin A 0%; Vitamin C 0%; Calcium 2%; Iron 4% **Exchanges:** ½ Starch, 1½ Other Carbohydrate, ½ High-Fat Meat, 2½ Fat **Carbohydrate Choices:** 2

caramel cream sandwich cookies

30 SANDWICH COOKIES

PREP TIME: *1 hour 15 minutes*

START TO FINISH: *1 hour 15 minutes*

HELEN BECKMAN

Mt. Vernon, IA

Bake-Off® Contest 06, 1954

1 In large bowl, beat brown sugar and 1 cup butter with electric mixer on medium speed, scraping bowl occasionally, until light and fluffy. Beat in egg yolk. On low speed, beat in flour until well blended. If necessary, cover with plastic wrap and refrigerate 15 minutes for easier handling.

2 Heat oven to 325°F. Shape dough into 1-inch balls. Place 2 inches apart on ungreased cookie sheets. With fork dipped in flour, flatten each ball until 1½-inch round.

3 Bake 10 to 14 minutes or until light golden brown. Cool 1 minute; remove from cookie sheets to cooling racks. Cool completely, about 15 minutes.

4 Meanwhile, in 2-quart saucepan, heat 2 tablespoons butter over medium heat, stirring constantly, until light golden brown. Remove from heat. Stir in remaining frosting ingredients, adding enough milk until smooth and spreadable.

5 Spread 1 teaspoon frosting between bottoms of pairs of cooled cookies.

High Altitude (3500–6500 ft): No change.

COOKIES

¾ cup packed brown sugar

1 cup butter, softened

1 egg yolk

2 cups Pillsbury BEST® all-purpose flour

FROSTING

2 tablespoons butter (do not use margarine)

1¼ cups powdered sugar

½ teaspoon vanilla

4 to 5 teaspoons milk

1 Sandwich Cookie: Calories 140 (Calories from Fat 60); Total Fat 7g (Saturated Fat 4.5g; Trans Fat 0g); Cholesterol 25mg; Sodium 50mg; Total Carbohydrate 17g (Dietary Fiber 0g; Sugars 10g); Protein 1g **% Daily Value:** Vitamin A 4%; Vitamin C 0%; Calcium 0%; Iron 2% **Exchanges:** ½ Starch, ½ Other Carbohydrate, 1½ Fat **Carbohydrate Choices:** 1

lemon light drop cookies

MR. DAVID CATO
San Antonio, TX
Bake-Off® Contest 29, 1980

6 DOZEN COOKIES

PREP TIME: *1 hour 10 minutes*
START TO FINISH: *1 hour 20 minutes*

1½ cups sugar

1 cup butter, softened, or shortening

1 container (6 oz) lemon burst low-fat
   yogurt or 1 cup sour cream

1 tablespoon grated lemon peel

1 teaspoon lemon extract

2 eggs

3½ cups Pillsbury BEST®
   all-purpose flour

2 teaspoons baking powder

½ teaspoon baking soda

½ teaspoon salt

Additional sugar (about 3 tablespoons)

1 Heat oven to 350°F. Grease cookie sheets with shortening or cooking spray. In large bowl, beat 1½ cups sugar and the butter with electric mixer on medium speed, scraping bowl occasionally, until light and fluffy. Beat in yogurt, lemon peel, lemon extract and eggs until well blended. On low speed, beat in flour, baking powder, baking soda and salt until dough forms. Let dough stand 10 minutes for easier handling.

2 Drop dough by rounded teaspoonfuls 2 inches apart onto cookie sheets. Sprinkle with additional sugar.

3 Bake 9 to 11 minutes or until edges are light golden brown. Immediately remove from cookie sheets to cooling racks. Cool completely, about 30 minutes. Store in airtight container.

High Altitude (3500–6500 ft): Decrease baking powder to 1 teaspoon.

1 Cookie: Calories 70 (Calories from Fat 25); Total Fat 3g (Saturated Fat 1.5g; Trans Fat 0g); Cholesterol 15mg; Sodium 60mg; Total Carbohydrate 10g (Dietary Fiber 0g; Sugars 5g); Protein 0g **% Daily Value:** Vitamin A 0%; Vitamin C 0%; Calcium 0%; Iron 0% **Exchanges:** 1 Other Carbohydrate, ½ Fat **Carbohydrate Choices:** ½

oatmeal-chip cookies

6 DOZEN COOKIES

PREP TIME: *1 hour 25 minutes*
START TO FINISH: *1 hour 25 minutes*

BETTYE J. STARK
Milwaukee, WI
Bake-Off® Contest 09, 1957

1 Heat oven to 375°F. In large bowl, beat sugars, butter and shortening with electric mixer on medium speed, scraping bowl occasionally, until light and fluffy. Beat in eggs. On low speed, beat in flour, baking soda and salt until well blended. Stir in oats, almonds and chocolate chips.

2 Drop dough by rounded teaspoonfuls 2 inches apart onto ungreased cookie sheets.

3 Bake 9 to 11 minutes or until light golden brown. Immediately remove from cookie sheets.

High Altitude (3500–6500 ft): No change.

1 cup granulated sugar

1 cup packed brown sugar

½ cup butter or margarine, softened

½ cup shortening

2 eggs

2 cups Pillsbury BEST® all-purpose flour

1 teaspoon baking soda

1 teaspoon salt

1½ cups quick-cooking oats

1 cup chopped almonds

1 cup semisweet chocolate chips (6 oz)

1 Cookie: Calories 90 (Calories from Fat 40); Total Fat 4.5g (Saturated Fat 1.5g; Trans Fat 0g); Cholesterol 10mg; Sodium 65mg; Total Carbohydrate 11g (Dietary Fiber 0g; Sugars 7g); Protein 1g **% Daily Value:** Vitamin A 0%; Vitamin C 0%; Calcium 0%; Iron 2% **Exchanges:** ½ Starch, 1 Fat **Carbohydrate Choices:** 1

lemon mardi gras squares

MRS. JOSEPH NEGROTTO
New Orleans, LA
Bake-Off® Contest 04, 1952

24 BARS

PREP TIME: *40 minutes*
START TO FINISH: *2 hours 15 minutes*

BARS

1½ cups Pillsbury BEST®
   all-purpose flour

½ teaspoon salt

¼ teaspoon baking powder

1 cup powdered sugar

1 cup granulated sugar

½ cup butter or margarine, softened

3 eggs

⅓ cup lemon juice

2 tablespoons grated lemon peel

½ cup chopped pecans

FROSTING

1 cup powdered sugar

2 tablespoons butter or margarine, softened

1 tablespoon half-and-half or milk

GARNISH

¼ cup chopped pecans

1. Heat oven to 400°F. Generously grease 13 × 9-inch pan with shortening or cooking spray; lightly flour. In small bowl, stir together flour, salt and baking powder; set aside.

2. In large bowl, beat powdered sugar, granulated sugar and butter with electric mixer on medium speed, scraping bowl occasionally, until blended. Beat in 1 egg at a time until blended. Beat 1 minute. On low speed, beat in flour mixture alternately with lemon juice, beginning and ending with flour mixture, until well blended. Stir in lemon peel and ½ cup pecans. Pour into pan.

3. Bake 22 to 27 minutes or until golden brown. Meanwhile, in small bowl, beat all frosting ingredients on low speed until smooth and spreadable.

4. Spread frosting over warm bars. Sprinkle with ¼ cup pecans. Cool completely in pan on cooling rack, about 1 hour. For bars, cut into 6 rows by 4 rows.

High Altitude (3500–6500 ft): No change.

1 Bar: Calories 180 (Calories from Fat 70); Total Fat 8g (Saturated Fat 3.5g; Trans Fat 0g); Cholesterol 40mg; Sodium 95mg; Total Carbohydrate 25g (Dietary Fiber 0g; Sugars 18g); Protein 2g **% Daily Value:** Vitamin A 4%; Vitamin C 0%; Calcium 0%; Iron 4% **Exchanges:** ½ Starch, 1 Other Carbohydrate, 1½ Fat **Carbohydrate Choices:** 1½

treasure chest bars

MRS. VIRGIL L. HAMMONS
Shawnee, KS
Bake-Off® Contest 14, 1962

48 BARS
PREP TIME: *30 minutes*
START TO FINISH: *2 hours*

BARS

2 cups Pillsbury BEST® all-purpose flour

½ cup granulated sugar

½ cup packed brown sugar

1½ teaspoons baking powder

Dash salt

½ cup butter, softened

¾ cup milk

1 teaspoon vanilla

2 eggs

3 bars (1.55 oz each) milk chocolate candy, cut into small pieces

1 cup maraschino cherries, drained, halved

1 cup coarsely chopped mixed nuts

FROSTING

¼ cup butter (do not use margarine)

2 cups powdered sugar

½ teaspoon vanilla

2 to 3 tablespoons milk

1 Heat oven to 350°F. Grease 15 × 10 × 1-inch pan with shortening or cooking spray. In large bowl, beat all bar ingredients except chocolate candy, cherries and nuts with electric mixer on medium speed 2 minutes, scraping bowl occasionally, until smooth. With spoon, stir in chocolate candy, cherries and nuts. Spread evenly in pan.

2 Bake 25 to 30 minutes or until light golden brown. Meanwhile, in 1-quart saucepan, heat ¼ cup butter over medium heat, stirring constantly, until light golden brown. Remove from heat. Stir in powdered sugar and ½ teaspoon vanilla. Stir in 2 to 3 tablespoons milk until smooth and spreadable.

3 Quickly spread frosting over warm bars. Cool completely in pan on cooling rack, about 1 hour. For bars, cut into 8 rows by 6 rows.

High Altitude (3500–6500 ft): No change.

1 Bar: Calories 130 (Calories from Fat 50); Total Fat 6g (Saturated Fat 2.5g; Trans Fat 0g); Cholesterol 15mg; Sodium 60mg; Total Carbohydrate 17g (Dietary Fiber 0g; Sugars 12g); Protein 2g **% Daily Value:** Vitamin A 2%; Vitamin C 0%; Calcium 2%; Iron 2% **Exchanges:** 1 Starch, 1 Fat **Carbohydrate Choices:** 1

charmin' cherry bars

DEANNA THOMPSON
Alexandria, MN
Bake-Off® Contest 03, 1951

24 BARS
PREP TIME: *15 minutes*
START TO FINISH: *1 hour 55 minutes*

CRUST

1 cup Pillsbury BEST® all-purpose flour
¼ cup powdered sugar
½ cup butter or margarine, softened

FILLING

¼ cup Pillsbury BEST® all-purpose flour
¾ cup granulated sugar
½ teaspoon baking powder
¼ teaspoon salt
2 eggs
½ cup maraschino cherries, well drained, chopped
½ cup coconut
½ cup chopped walnuts

1 Heat oven to 350°F. In small bowl, mix 1 cup flour and the powdered sugar. With fork or pastry blender, cut in butter until mixture resembles coarse crumbs. Press mixture firmly in bottom of ungreased 9-inch square pan.

2 Bake 10 minutes. Meanwhile, in same small bowl, mix ¼ cup flour, the granulated sugar, baking powder and salt. Add eggs; beat well with spoon. Stir in cherries, coconut and walnuts.

3 Spread cherry mixture over partially baked crust; bake 25 to 30 minutes longer or until golden brown. Cool completely in pan on cooling rack, about 1 hour. For bars, cut into 6 rows by 4 rows.

High Altitude (3500–6500 ft): No change.

1 Bar: Calories 130 (Calories from Fat 60); Total Fat 6g (Saturated Fat 3g; Trans Fat 0g); Cholesterol 30mg; Sodium 70mg; Total Carbohydrate 15g (Dietary Fiber 0g; Sugars 9g); Protein 2g **% Daily Value:** Vitamin A 2%; Vitamin C 0%; Calcium 0%; Iron 2% **Exchanges:** ½ Starch, ½ Other Carbohydrate, 1 Fat **Carbohydrate Choices:** 1

chewy peanut brownie bars

48 BARS

PREP TIME: *15 minutes*

START TO FINISH: *3 hours 35 minutes*

HELEN PEACH
Pensacola, FL
Bake-Off® Contest 34, 1990

1 Heat oven to 350°F. In large bowl, mix all crust ingredients. Press mixture evenly in bottom of ungreased 15 × 10 × 1-inch pan.

2 In small bowl, beat corn syrup and peanut butter with electric mixer on low speed until well blended. Beat in 1 tablespoon melted butter and ½ teaspoon vanilla. Stir in peanuts. Spread filling evenly over crust to within ½ inch of edges.

3 Bake 18 to 20 minutes or until edges are firm and center is just firm to the touch. Cool completely in pan on cooling rack, about 1 hour.

4 In 1-quart saucepan, heat 1 tablespoon butter, the chocolate and water over low heat, stirring constantly, until butter and chocolate are melted and mixture is smooth. With wire whisk, stir in powdered sugar and ½ teaspoon vanilla until smooth. Drizzle glaze over cooled brownies. Let stand until glaze is set, about 2 hours. For bars, cut into 8 rows by 6 rows.

High Altitude (3500–6500 ft): Add ¼ cup all-purpose flour to dry brownie mix.

CRUST
1 box (19.5 oz) Pillsbury® traditional
    fudge brownie mix
½ cup butter or margarine, melted
1 egg

FILLING
1 cup dark or light corn syrup
¾ cup peanut butter
1 tablespoon butter or
    margarine, melted
½ teaspoon vanilla
1 cup unsalted peanuts

GLAZE
1 tablespoon butter or margarine
1 oz unsweetened baking chocolate,
    cut into pieces
2 tablespoons plus 1½ teaspoons water
1 cup powdered sugar
½ teaspoon vanilla

1 Bar: Calories 150 (Calories from Fat 70); Total Fat 7g (Saturated Fat 2.5g; Trans Fat 0g); Cholesterol 10mg; Sodium 75mg; Total Carbohydrate 19g (Dietary Fiber 1g; Sugars 12g); Protein 3g **% Daily Value:** Vitamin A 0%; Vitamin C 0%; Calcium 0%; Iron 4% **Exchanges:** 1 Starch, 1½ Fat **Carbohydrate Choices:** 1

guess-again candy crunch

PAT PARSONS
Bakersfield, CA
Bake-Off® Contest 39, 2000

50 PIECES

PREP TIME: *30 minutes*
START TO FINISH: *30 minutes*

½ cup white chocolate candy melts or coating wafers*

½ cup peanut butter

1 cup plain dry bread crumbs

1 cup light or dark chocolate candy melts for candy making*

¼ cup dry-roasted peanuts, finely chopped

1 Line cookie sheet with waxed paper. In small microwavable bowl, mix white chocolate candy melts and peanut butter; microwave on Medium 2 minutes. Stir until smooth; stir in bread crumbs. Place mixture on cookie sheet. Top with another sheet of waxed paper; pat or roll into ¼-inch-thick rectangle. Remove top waxed paper.

2 In small microwavable bowl, microwave ½ cup of the light chocolate candy melts on Medium 2 minutes. Stir until smooth; spread evenly over peanut butter layer. Sprinkle with 2 tablespoons of the peanuts. Freeze 5 minutes or refrigerate 15 minutes to set chocolate.

3 In same small microwavable bowl, microwave remaining ½ cup light chocolate candy melts on Medium 2 minutes. Stir until smooth.

4 Remove candy from freezer. Turn candy over; remove waxed paper. Spread light chocolate over peanut butter layer. Immediately sprinkle with remaining 2 tablespoons peanuts; press in lightly. Refrigerate until firm, about 10 minutes. Break or cut into small pieces. Store in refrigerator; serve cold.

High Altitude (3500–6500 ft): No change.

*Chopped vanilla-flavored and chocolate-flavored candy coating, or white vanilla baking chips and semisweet chocolate chips, can be substituted for the white and light or dark chocolate candy melts.

1 Piece: Calories 60 (Calories from Fat 35); Total Fat 3.5g (Saturated Fat 1.5g; Trans Fat 0g); Cholesterol 0mg; Sodium 40mg; Total Carbohydrate 6g (Dietary Fiber 0g; Sugars 4g); Protein 2g **% Daily Value:** Vitamin A 0%; Vitamin C 0%; Calcium 0%; Iron 0% **Exchanges:** ½ Starch, ½ Fat **Carbohydrate Choices:** ½

hoosier peanut bars

EDGAR L. BLEEKE
Fort Wayne, IN
Bake-Off® Contest 01, 1949

24 BARS
PREP TIME: *15 minutes*
START TO FINISH: *1 hour 50 minutes*

BASE

2 cups Pillsbury BEST® all-purpose flour

2 teaspoons baking powder

1 teaspoon baking soda

½ teaspoon salt

½ cup granulated sugar

½ cup packed brown sugar

½ cup shortening

1 teaspoon vanilla

2 egg yolks

3 tablespoons cold water

TOPPING

1 cup semisweet chocolate chips (6 oz)

2 egg whites

1 cup packed brown sugar

¾ cup chopped salted peanuts

1 Heat oven to 325°F. Grease 1 (15 × 10 × 1-inch) pan or 2 (8-inch) square pans with shortening or cooking spray; lightly flour. In small bowl, stir together flour, baking powder, baking soda and salt; set aside.

2 In large bowl, beat granulated sugar, ½ cup brown sugar and the shortening with electric mixer on medium speed, scraping bowl occasionally, until blended. Beat in vanilla and egg yolks. On low speed, beat in flour mixture alternately with cold water until dough forms (dough will be stiff). Press dough in pan(s).

3 Sprinkle chocolate chips over dough; press in lightly. In small bowl, beat egg whites on medium speed until foamy. Gradually beat in 1 cup brown sugar until stiff. Spread over chocolate chips. Sprinkle with peanuts.

4 Bake 30 to 35 minutes or until light golden brown. Let stand about 10 minutes. While warm, cut 15 × 10 × 1-inch pan into 6 rows by 4 rows or cut each square pan into 4 rows by 3 rows. Cool 1 hour.

High Altitude (3500–6500 ft): No change.

1 Bar: Calories 220 (Calories from Fat 80); Total Fat 9g (Saturated Fat 3g; Trans Fat 0.5g); Cholesterol 15mg; Sodium 170mg; Total Carbohydrate 31g (Dietary Fiber 1g; Sugars 21g); Protein 3g **% Daily Value:** Vitamin A 0%; Vitamin C 0%; Calcium 4%; Iron 6% **Exchanges:** 1 Starch, 1 Other Carbohydrate, 1½ Fat **Carbohydrate Choices:** 2

marshmallow-fudge bars

24 BARS

PREP TIME: *30 minutes*

START TO FINISH: *1 hour 45 minutes*

MRS. ELMER ELLIS MOORING

Dallas, TX

Bake-Off® Contest 01, 1949

1 Heat oven to 350°F. Grease 13 × 9-inch pan with shortening or cooking spray; lightly flour. In small bowl, stir together flour, baking powder, salt and cocoa; set aside.

2 In large bowl, beat shortening and granulated sugar with electric mixer on medium speed, scraping bowl occasionally, until blended. Add eggs, one at a time, beating well after each addition. Beat in 1 teaspoon vanilla. On low speed, beat in flour mixture until well blended. Stir in pecans. Spread batter in pan.

3 Bake 22 to 24 minutes or until center is set and edges are light golden brown. Cut marshmallows in half; cover top of baked bars with marshmallow halves, cut sides down. Bake 3 minutes longer or until marshmallows are soft.

4 Spread marshmallows evenly with metal spatula. Cool completely in pan on cooling rack, about 1 hour.

5 In 1½-quart saucepan, heat brown sugar, water and chocolate to boiling over medium heat. Cook 3 minutes, stirring constantly. Stir in butter and 1 teaspoon vanilla. Cool 15 minutes. With electric mixer on medium speed, beat in powdered sugar until smooth. If necessary, add milk, 1 teaspoon at a time, until frosting is thin enough to spread. Spread frosting over marshmallow topping. For bars, cut into 6 rows by 4 rows.

High Altitude (3500–6500 ft): No change.

BARS

¾ cup Pillsbury BEST® all-purpose flour

¼ teaspoon baking powder

¼ teaspoon salt

2 tablespoons unsweetened baking cocoa

½ cup shortening

¾ cup granulated sugar

2 eggs

1 teaspoon vanilla

½ cup chopped pecans

12 large marshmallows

FROSTING

½ cup packed brown sugar

¼ cup water

2 oz unsweetened baking chocolate

3 tablespoons butter or margarine

1 teaspoon vanilla

1½ cups powdered sugar

3 to 4 teaspoons milk

1 Bar: Calories 190 (Calories from Fat 80); Total Fat 9g (Saturated Fat 3g; Trans Fat 1g); Cholesterol 20mg; Sodium 50mg; Total Carbohydrate 25g (Dietary Fiber 0g; Sugars 20g); Protein 2g **% Daily Value:** Vitamin A 0%; Vitamin C 0%; Calcium 0%; Iron 4% **Exchanges:** ½ Starch, 1 Other Carbohydrate, 2 Fat **Carbohydrate Choices:** 1½

nut nibblers

RACHEL HEDRICK
New Smyrna Beach, FL
Bake-Off® Contest 17, 1966

48 BARS
PREP TIME: *35 minutes*
START TO FINISH: *2 hours*

4 eggs
1 cup sugar
1 cup Pillsbury BEST® all-purpose flour
1 teaspoon vanilla
2½ cups finely chopped pitted dates
1 cup toasted whole-grain oat cereal
1 cup bite-size squares crisp rice cereal, broken
1 cup pretzel sticks, broken into ½-inch pieces
1 cup chopped walnuts

1 Heat oven to 350°F. Grease bottom only of 15 × 10 × 1-inch pan with shortening or cooking spray; lightly flour. In large bowl, beat eggs with electric mixer on high speed until light and fluffy. Gradually beat in sugar, scraping bowl occasionally, until thick and lemon colored. On medium speed, beat in flour and vanilla until well blended. Stir in dates.

2 In medium bowl, mix remaining ingredients. Reserve 1 cup for topping. Stir remaining cereal mixture into batter. Spread in pan. Sprinkle reserved cereal mixture evenly over top.

3 Bake 20 to 25 minutes or until top springs back when touched midway from edge to center. Cool completely in pan on cooling rack, about 1 hour. For bars, cut into 8 rows by 6 rows.

High Altitude (3500–6500 ft): No change.

1 Bar: Calories 90 (Calories from Fat 20); Total Fat 2g (Saturated Fat 0g; Trans Fat 0g); Cholesterol 20mg; Sodium 30mg; Total Carbohydrate 15g (Dietary Fiber 1g; Sugars 10g); Protein 2g **% Daily Value:** Vitamin A 0%; Vitamin C 0%; Calcium 0%; Iron 4% **Exchanges:** ½ Starch, ½ Other Carbohydrate, ½ Fat **Carbohydrate Choices:** 1

coconut-lemon-crescent bars

MS. MARILYN BLANKSCHIEN
Clintonville, WI
Bake-Off® Contest 30, 1982

36 BARS

PREP TIME: *15 minutes*
START TO FINISH: *1 hour 5 minutes*

CRUST
1 can (8 oz) Pillsbury® refrigerated
   crescent dinner rolls

FILLING
2 eggs, slightly beaten
1 cup sugar
1 cup flaked coconut
2 tablespoons Pillsbury BEST®
   all-purpose flour
½ teaspoon baking powder
½ teaspoon grated lemon peel
¼ teaspoon salt
2 tablespoons lemon juice
2 tablespoons butter or
   margarine, melted

1   Heat oven to 375°F. Unroll dough into 2 long rectangles. Place in ungreased 13 × 9-inch pan; press in bottom and ½ inch up sides to form crust, firmly pressing perforations to seal.

2   Bake 5 minutes. Meanwhile, in medium bowl, mix all filling ingredients until well blended.

3   Pour filling over partially baked crust; bake 12 to 17 minutes longer or until light golden brown. Cool completely in pan on cooling rack, about 30 minutes. For bars, cut into 6 rows by 6 rows.

High Altitude (3500–6500 ft): Bake 14 to 19 minutes.

1 Bar: Calories 70 (Calories from Fat 25); Total Fat 3g (Saturated Fat 1.5g; Trans Fat 0g); Cholesterol 15mg; Sodium 85mg; Total Carbohydrate 9g (Dietary Fiber 0g; Sugars 7g); Protein 0g **% Daily Value:** Vitamin A 0%; Vitamin C 0%; Calcium 0%; Iron 0% **Exchanges:** ½ Starch, ½ Fat **Carbohydrate Choices:** ½

spicy banana bars

MRS. BYARD CUMMINGS
Enderlin, ND
Bake-Off® Contest 06, 1954

36 BARS

PREP TIME: *15 minutes*
START TO FINISH: *1 hour*

BARS

¼ cup butter, softened, or shortening

⅓ cup mashed ripe banana
(1 to 2 small)

¼ cup milk

1 egg

1 cup Pillsbury BEST® all-purpose flour

¾ cup granulated sugar

½ teaspoon baking powder

½ teaspoon salt

¼ teaspoon baking soda

¾ teaspoon ground cinnamon

¼ teaspoon ground cloves

¼ teaspoon ground allspice

⅓ cup chopped pecans

FROSTING

2 tablespoons butter or margarine

1 cup powdered sugar

2 teaspoons lemon juice

2 to 4 teaspoons water

1 Heat oven to 350°F. Grease 13 × 9-inch pan with shortening or cooking spray; lightly flour. In small bowl, beat ¼ cup butter and the banana with electric mixer on medium speed, scraping bowl occasionally, until blended. Beat in milk and egg. On low speed, beat in remaining bar ingredients, scraping bowl occasionally, until well blended. Spread batter in pan.

2 Bake 20 to 25 minutes or until light golden brown. Meanwhile, in 1-quart saucepan, melt 2 tablespoons butter. Stir in powdered sugar, lemon juice and enough water until frosting is smooth and spreadable.

3 Spread frosting over warm bars. Cool completely in pan on cooling rack, about 30 minutes. For bars, cut into 6 rows by 6 rows.

High Altitude (3500–6500 ft): Decrease granulated sugar to ⅔ cup.

1 Bar: Calories 70 (Calories from Fat 25); Total Fat 3g (Saturated Fat 1.5g; Trans Fat 0g); Cholesterol 10mg; Sodium 65mg; Total Carbohydrate 11g (Dietary Fiber 0g; Sugars 8g); Protein 0g **% Daily Value:** Vitamin A 0%; Vitamin C 0%; Calcium 0%; Iron 0% **Exchanges:** 1 Other Carbohydrate, ½ Fat **Carbohydrate Choices:** 1

White Chocolate-Almond Brownies (page 123) ▶

triple-espresso brownies

SHERYL HAKKO

Eugene, OR

Bake-Off® Contest 34, 1990

48 BROWNIES

PREP TIME: *20 minutes*

START TO FINISH: *1 hour 50 minutes*

BROWNIES

1 box (19.5 oz) Pillsbury® traditional fudge brownie mix

½ cup vegetable oil

¼ cup water

2 eggs

2 teaspoons instant espresso coffee granules

1 teaspoon vanilla

FILLING

¼ cup butter or margarine, softened

½ cup packed brown sugar

1 egg

2 teaspoons instant espresso coffee granules

1 teaspoon vanilla

1 cup coarsely chopped walnuts

2 bars (5 oz each) sweet dark baking chocolate or 1 bar (9.7 oz) semisweet dark baking chocolate, chopped

GLAZE

½ cup semisweet chocolate chips

1 tablespoon butter or margarine

⅛ teaspoon instant espresso coffee granules

1 to 2 teaspoons milk or whipping cream

1 Heat oven to 350°F. Grease bottom only of 13 × 9-inch pan with shortening or cooking spray. In large bowl, beat all brownie ingredients 50 strokes with spoon. Spread in pan. Bake 28 minutes. Remove from oven.

2 Meanwhile, in small bowl, beat ¼ cup butter and the brown sugar with electric mixer on medium speed until light and fluffy. Add 1 egg, 2 teaspoons coffee granules and 1 teaspoon vanilla; beat until well blended. In medium bowl, mix walnuts and chopped chocolate. With spoon, stir in brown sugar mixture until well blended.

3 Spoon and carefully spread filling over baked brownies. Bake 17 to 20 minutes longer or until light brown.

4 In 1-quart saucepan, melt chocolate chips and 1 tablespoon butter over low heat, stirring constantly, until smooth. Remove from heat. With wire whisk, stir in ⅛ teaspoon coffee granules and enough milk for desired drizzling consistency. Drizzle over warm brownies. Cool completely, about 45 minutes. For brownies, cut into 8 rows by 6 rows.

High Altitude (3500–6500 ft): Add ½ cup all-purpose flour to dry brownie mix. Increase water to ⅓ cup.

1 Brownie: Calories 150 (Calories from Fat 80); Total Fat 9g (Saturated Fat 3g; Trans Fat 0g); Cholesterol 15mg; Sodium 45mg; Total Carbohydrate 17g (Dietary Fiber 1g; Sugars 13g); Protein 2g **% Daily Value:** Vitamin A 0%; Vitamin C 0%; Calcium 0%; Iron 4% **Exchanges:** 1 Other Carbohydrate, 2 Fat **Carbohydrate Choices:** 1

peanut butter 'n fudge brownies

JEANNIE HOBEL
San Diego, CA
Bake-Off® Contest 31, 1984

36 BROWNIES

PREP TIME: *45 minutes*
START TO FINISH: *2 hours 35 minutes*

CHOCOLATE PORTION

1½ cups Pillsbury BEST®
   all-purpose flour

¾ cup unsweetened baking cocoa

1 teaspoon baking powder

½ teaspoon salt

2 cups granulated sugar

1 cup butter or margarine, softened

4 eggs

2 teaspoons vanilla

1 cup peanut butter chips (6 oz)

PEANUT BUTTER PORTION

¾ cup peanut butter

⅓ cup butter or margarine, softened

⅓ cup granulated sugar

2 tablespoons Pillsbury BEST®
   all-purpose flour

¾ teaspoon vanilla

2 eggs

FROSTING

3 oz unsweetened baking chocolate

3 tablespoons butter or margarine

2⅔ cups powdered sugar

¼ teaspoon salt

¾ teaspoon vanilla

4 to 5 tablespoons water

1 Heat oven to 350°F. Grease 13 × 9-inch pan with shortening or cooking spray. In small bowl, mix 1½ cups flour, the cocoa, baking powder and ½ teaspoon salt; set aside.

2 In large bowl, beat 2 cups granulated sugar and 1 cup butter with electric mixer on medium speed, scraping bowl occasionally, until light and fluffy. Add 4 eggs, one at a time, beating well after each addition. Beat in 2 teaspoons vanilla. On low speed, gradually beat in flour mixture until well blended. Stir in peanut butter chips.

3 In small bowl, beat peanut butter and ⅓ cup butter on medium speed until smooth. Beat in ⅓ cup granulated sugar and 2 tablespoons flour. Beat in ¾ teaspoon vanilla and 2 eggs until well blended. Spread half of chocolate mixture in pan. Spread peanut butter mixture evenly over chocolate mixture. Spread remaining chocolate mixture evenly over peanut butter mixture. To marble, pull knife through layers in wide curves.

4 Bake 40 to 50 minutes or until top springs back when touched lightly in center and brownies begin to pull away from sides of pan. Cool completely, about 1 hour.

5 In 2-quart saucepan, melt chocolate and 3 tablespoons butter over low heat, stirring constantly, until smooth. Remove from heat. Stir in powdered sugar, ¼ teaspoon salt, ¾ teaspoon vanilla and enough water for desired spreading consistency. Frost brownies. For brownies, cut into 6 rows by 6 rows.

High Altitude (3500–6500 ft): No change.

1 Brownie: Calories 270 (Calories from Fat 130); Total Fat 14g (Saturated Fat 7g; Trans Fat 0g); Cholesterol 55mg; Sodium 170mg; Total Carbohydrate 31g (Dietary Fiber 1g; Sugars 24g); Protein 4g **% Daily Value:** Vitamin A 6%; Vitamin C 0%; Calcium 2%; Iron 6% **Exchanges:** 2 Other Carbohydrate, ½ High-Fat Meat, 2 Fat **Carbohydrate Choices:** 2

sugar cookie–chocolate crunch fudge

48 CANDIES

PREP TIME: *15 minutes*

START TO FINISH: *2 hours 15 minutes*

DICK BOULANGER

Williston, VT

Bake-Off® Contest 42, 2006

1 In 3-quart heavy saucepan or deep 10-inch nonstick skillet, cook corn syrup, butter, salt and milk over medium heat 2 to 3 minutes, stirring constantly with wooden spoon, until well blended. Reduce heat to medium-low; stir in cookie dough chunks. Cook 3 to 5 minutes, stirring constantly, until mixture is smooth and candy thermometer reads 160°F. Remove from heat.

2 Stir in chocolate chips and vanilla until chips are melted and mixture is smooth. Add crushed granola bars; stir until well blended. Cook over low heat 1 to 2 minutes, stirring constantly, until mixture is shiny. Spread in ungreased 12 × 8-inch or 13 × 9-inch pan.** Refrigerate uncovered at least 2 hours until firm.

3 For serving pieces, cut into 8 rows by 6 rows. Serve in decorative candy cups or mini paper baking cups on platter garnished with mint sprigs.

High Altitude (3500–6500 ft): No change.

2 tablespoons light corn syrup

2 tablespoons butter or margarine

¼ teaspoon salt

1 can (14 oz) sweetened condensed milk (not evaporated)

1 roll (16.5 oz) Pillsbury® Create 'n Bake™ refrigerated sugar cookies, cut into small chunks

2 bags (12 oz each) semisweet chocolate chips (4 cups)

5 teaspoons vanilla

6 pecan crunch crunchy granola bars (3 pouches from 8.9-oz box), coarsely crushed (heaping 1 cup)*

Fresh mint sprigs, if desired

*To easily crush granola bars, do not unwrap; use rolling pin to crush bars.

**To easily cut fudge, line pan with foil so foil extends over sides of pan. Lift candy from pan using foil.

1 Candy: Calories 170 (Calories from Fat 70); Total Fat 8g (Saturated Fat 4g; Trans Fat 0.5g); Cholesterol 5mg; Sodium 65mg; Total Carbohydrate 22g (Dietary Fiber 0g; Sugars 16g); Protein 2g **% Daily Value:** Vitamin A 0%; Vitamin C 0%; Calcium 2%; Iron 4% **Exchanges:** ½ Starch, 1 Other Carbohydrate, 1½ Fat **Carbohydrate Choices:** 1½

black and white brownies

PENELOPE WEISS

Pleasant Grove, UT

Bake-Off® Contest 35, 1992

36 BROWNIES

PREP TIME: *15 minutes*

START TO FINISH: *2 hours 30 minutes*

BROWNIES

1 box (19.5 oz) Pillsbury® traditional
  fudge brownie mix

¼ cup water

½ cup vegetable oil

2 eggs

1½ cups chopped pecans

1 cup semisweet chocolate chips (6 oz)

1 bag (12 oz) white vanilla baking chips
  (2 cups)

FROSTING

2 cups powdered sugar

¼ cup unsweetened baking cocoa

3 to 4 tablespoons hot water

¼ cup butter or margarine, melted

1 teaspoon vanilla

½ to 1 cup pecan halves

1 Heat oven to 350°F. Grease bottom only of 13 × 9-inch pan with shortening or cooking spray. In large bowl, beat brownie mix, ¼ cup water, the oil and eggs 50 strokes with spoon. Stir in chopped pecans, chocolate chips and 1 cup of the vanilla baking chips. Spread in pan.

2 Bake 28 to 34 minutes or until center is set. Remove from oven; immediately sprinkle with remaining 1 cup vanilla baking chips. Let stand 1 minute to soften chips; spread evenly over brownies.

3 In small bowl, beat all frosting ingredients except pecan halves with electric mixer on medium speed until smooth (mixture will be thin). Spoon over melted vanilla baking chips; spread to cover. Arrange pecan halves on frosting. Cool completely, about 1 hour 30 minutes. For brownies, cut into 6 rows by 6 rows.

High Altitude (3500–6500 ft): Add ½ cup all-purpose flour to dry brownie mix. Increase water in brownies to ⅓ cup.

1 Brownie: Calories 260 (Calories from Fat 130); Total Fat 14g (Saturated Fat 5g; Trans Fat 0g); Cholesterol 15mg; Sodium 75mg; Total Carbohydrate 29g (Dietary Fiber 1g; Sugars 24g); Protein 2g **% Daily Value:** Vitamin A 0%; Vitamin C 0%; Calcium 2%; Iron 6% **Exchanges:** 2 Other Carbohydrate, 3 Fat **Carbohydrate Choices:** 2

caramel swirl cheesecake brownies

24 BROWNIES

PREP TIME: *30 minutes*

START TO FINISH: *2 hours 45 minutes*

REBECCA MOE
Carmichael, CA
Bake-Off® Contest 36, 1994

1 Heat oven to 325°F. Grease bottom only of 13 × 9-inch pan with shortening or cooking spray. In large bowl, beat all base ingredients with spoon until dough forms. Press lightly in bottom of pan.

2 In large bowl, beat cream cheese and ⅓ cup peanut butter with electric mixer on low speed until smooth. Add granulated sugar, flour, sour cream and vanilla; beat until blended. Add 2 eggs, one at a time, beating just until blended. Pour filling over base.

3 In 1-quart heavy saucepan, cook caramels and 3 tablespoons whipping cream over low heat, stirring constantly, until caramels are melted and mixture is smooth. Drop spoonfuls of caramel sauce randomly over filling. For swirl design, pull knife through batter in wide curves; turn pan and repeat.

4 Bake 35 to 45 minutes or until center is set and edges are light golden brown. Cool in pan on cooling rack 30 minutes. Refrigerate 1 hour before serving. For brownies, cut into 6 rows by 4 rows. Store in refrigerator.

High Altitude (3500–6500 ft): Add 2 tablespoons all-purpose flour to dry brownie mix.

BASE

1 box (19.5 oz) Pillsbury® traditional fudge brownie mix

½ cup butter or margarine, softened

¼ cup creamy peanut butter

1 egg

FILLING

2 packages (8 oz each) cream cheese, softened

⅓ cup creamy peanut butter

1 cup granulated sugar

3 tablespoons Pillsbury BEST® all-purpose flour

¼ cup sour cream

2 teaspoons vanilla

2 eggs

CARAMEL SAUCE

12 caramels, unwrapped

3 tablespoons whipping cream

1 Brownie: Calories 320 (Calories from Fat 160); Total Fat 18g (Saturated Fat 9g; Trans Fat 0g); Cholesterol 60mg; Sodium 200mg; Total Carbohydrate 34g (Dietary Fiber 1g; Sugars 25g); Protein 5g **% Daily Value:** Vitamin A 8%; Vitamin C 0%; Calcium 4%; Iron 8% **Exchanges:** ½ Starch, 2 Other Carbohydrate, ½ High-Fat Meat, 2½ Fat **Carbohydrate Choices:** 2

missouri waltz brownies

MRS. NATALIE TOWNES
Kriksville, MO
Bake-Off® Contest 02, 1950

20 BROWNIES

PREP TIME: *45 minutes*
START TO FINISH: *2 hours 50 minutes*

BROWNIES

¾ cup Pillsbury BEST® all-purpose flour
½ teaspoon baking powder
½ teaspoon salt
½ cup shortening
1 cup granulated sugar
2 eggs
2½ oz unsweetened baking chocolate, melted, cooled
1 teaspoon vanilla
½ cup chopped nuts

MINT CREAM FROSTING

1½ cups powdered sugar
½ cup half-and-half or evaporated milk
1 tablespoon butter or margarine
¼ teaspoon peppermint extract
1 drop green food color
2 oz unsweetened baking chocolate, melted, cooled

1 Heat oven to 350°F. Grease 9-inch square pan with shortening or cooking spray; lightly flour. In small bowl, stir together flour, baking powder and salt; set aside.

2 In medium bowl, beat shortening and granulated sugar with electric mixer on medium speed, scraping bowl occasionally, until well blended. Beat in eggs, 2½ oz melted chocolate and the vanilla. On low speed, beat in flour mixture and nuts until well blended. Pour into pan.

3 Bake 20 to 30 minutes or until toothpick inserted in center comes out clean. Cool completely, about 1 hour.

4 In 1½-quart saucepan, mix powdered sugar and half-and-half. Cook over medium heat about 10 minutes until a small amount of mixture dropped into a cupful of very cold water forms a soft ball that flattens between fingers (232°F). Remove from heat. Stir in butter. Cool to lukewarm (120°F). Add peppermint extract and food color; beat on medium speed until thick and creamy. Spread over brownies.

5 Spread 2 oz melted chocolate over frosting. Let stand about 45 minutes or until chocolate is set. For brownies, cut into 5 rows by 4 rows. Store in refrigerator.

High Altitude (3500–6500 ft): Bake 25 to 30 minutes.

1 Brownie: Calories 220 (Calories from Fat 110); Total Fat 12g (Saturated Fat 4.5g; Trans Fat 1g); Cholesterol 25mg; Sodium 85mg; Total Carbohydrate 25g (Dietary Fiber 1g; Sugars 19g); Protein 3g **% Daily Value:** Vitamin A 0%; Vitamin C 0%; Calcium 2%; Iron 8% **Exchanges:** ½ Starch, 1 Other Carbohydrate, 2½ Fat **Carbohydrate Choices:** 1½

bonbon brownies

MRS. O. C. JACK
New Orleans, LA
Bake-Off® Contest 03, 1951

25 BROWNIES

PREP TIME: *25 minutes*
START TO FINISH: *1 hour 55 minutes*

BROWNIES

⅔ cup Pillsbury BEST® all-purpose flour

¼ cup unsweetened baking cocoa

½ teaspoon baking powder

¼ teaspoon salt

½ cup shortening

¾ cup sugar

1 whole egg

1 egg yolk

1 teaspoon vanilla

¼ cup chopped pecans

MERINGUE

1 egg white

¼ teaspoon cream of tartar

¼ cup sugar

¼ cup chopped pecans

1 Heat oven to 350°F. Generously grease 8-inch square pan with shortening or cooking spray.

2 In small bowl, stir together flour, cocoa, baking powder and salt; set aside. In medium bowl, beat shortening and ¾ cup sugar with electric mixer on medium speed until blended. Beat in whole egg, egg yolk and vanilla. On low speed, beat in flour mixture and ¼ cup pecans until well blended. Spread in pan.

3 In small bowl, beat egg white and cream of tartar on high speed until foamy. Add gradually ¼ cup sugar, beating constantly, until mixture stands in stiff, lustrous peaks when beater is raised. Fold ¼ cup chopped pecans into meringue; spread over batter.

4 Bake 30 to 35 minutes or until lightly browned. Cool completely, about 1 hour. For brownies, cut into 5 rows by 5 rows.

High Altitude (3500–6500 ft): Use 2 eggs in brownie batter instead of 1 egg and 1 yolk. Bake 35 to 40 minutes.

1 Brownie: Calories 110 (Calories from Fat 60); Total Fat 6g (Saturated Fat 1.5g; Trans Fat 0.5g); Cholesterol 15mg; Sodium 40mg; Total Carbohydrate 11g (Dietary Fiber 0g; Sugars 8g); Protein 1g **% Daily Value:** Vitamin A 0%; Vitamin C 0%; Calcium 0%; Iron 2% **Exchanges:** 1 Other Carbohydrate, 1 Fat **Carbohydrate Choices:** 1

snowcap brownies

24 BROWNIES

PREP TIME: *30 minutes*
START TO FINISH: *2 hours 10 minutes*

JUDITH A. HARPER
Los Angeles, CA
Bake-Off® Contest 10, 1958

1 Heat oven to 325°F. Generously grease 15 × 10 × 1-inch pan with shortening or cooking spray.

2 In small bowl, stir together flour, baking powder and salt; set aside. In 2-quart saucepan, melt butter and chocolate over low heat, stirring frequently; cool 20 minutes. Stir in 1¼ cups sugar, 1 teaspoon vanilla and the food color. Add eggs and egg yolk; beat with spoon until well blended. Stir in flour mixture and nuts. Spread in pan.

3 In small bowl, beat egg white with electric mixer on high speed until stiff peaks form. Beat in ½ cup sugar and ½ teaspoon vanilla. Drop meringue by teaspoonfuls onto brownie batter. Draw tip of knife or metal spatula through batter lengthwise, then crosswise, to give meringue a design.

4 Bake 25 to 30 minutes or until meringue is light brown and edges are firm to the touch. Cool completely, about 1 hour. For brownies, cut into 6 rows by 4 rows.

High Altitude (3500–6500 ft): Bake 22 to 27 minutes.

BROWNIES
¾ cup Pillsbury BEST® all-purpose flour
1 teaspoon baking powder
½ teaspoon salt
½ cup butter or margarine
2½ oz unsweetened baking chocolate
1¼ cups sugar
1 teaspoon vanilla
½ teaspoon red food color
2 whole eggs
1 egg yolk
1 cup chopped nuts

MERINGUE
1 egg white
½ cup sugar
½ teaspoon vanilla

1 Brownie: Calories 170 (Calories from Fat 80); Total Fat 9g (Saturated Fat 4g; Trans Fat 0g); Cholesterol 35mg; Sodium 105mg; Total Carbohydrate 19g (Dietary Fiber 0g; Sugars 15g); Protein 2g **% Daily Value:** Vitamin A 4%; Vitamin C 0%; Calcium 2%; Iron 6% **Exchanges:** ½ Starch, 1 Other Carbohydrate, 1½ Fat **Carbohydrate Choices:** 1

almond-toffee-mocha squares

BEVERLY STARR
Nashville, AR
Bake-Off® Contest 41, 2004

24 BROWNIES
PREP TIME: *20 minutes*
START TO FINISH: *2 hours 50 minutes*

BROWNIES

1 box (19.5 oz) Pillsbury® fudge toffee
or traditional fudge brownie mix

1 teaspoon instant coffee granules
or crystals

½ cup butter or margarine, melted

¼ cup water

2 eggs

½ cup finely chopped chocolate-
covered English toffee candy bars
(two 1.4-oz bars)

½ cup slivered almonds, toasted*

TOPPING

4 oz cream cheese (half of 8-oz
package), softened

⅓ cup packed brown sugar

1 teaspoon instant coffee granules
or crystals

1½ cups whipping cream

1 teaspoon vanilla

1 cup chopped chocolate-covered
English toffee candy bars
(four 1.4-oz bars)

½ cup slivered almonds, toasted*

*To toast almonds, bake uncovered in ungreased shallow pan in 350°F oven 6 to 10 minutes, stirring occasionally, until light brown.

1 Heat oven to 350°F. Grease bottom only of 13 × 9-inch pan with shortening or cooking spray. In large bowl, beat brownie mix, 1 teaspoon coffee granules, the butter, water and eggs with electric mixer on low speed 1 minute. Gently stir in ½ cup chopped candy bars and ½ cup almonds. Spread batter in pan.

2 Bake 24 to 28 minutes or until edges are firm. DO NOT OVERBAKE. Cool completely in pan on wire rack, about 1 hour.

3 In medium bowl, beat cream cheese, brown sugar and 1 teaspoon coffee granules on medium speed until smooth. On high speed, beat in whipping cream and vanilla until soft peaks form.

4 Spread cream cheese mixture over cooled brownies. Sprinkle 1 cup chopped candy bars and ½ cup almonds over top. Refrigerate at least 1 hour before serving. For brownies, cut into 6 rows by 4 rows. Store in refrigerator.

High Altitude (3500–6500 ft): Follow High Altitude directions on brownie mix box. Bake 28 to 32 minutes.

1 Brownie: Calories 300 (Calories from Fat 160); Total Fat 18g (Saturated Fat 9g; Trans Fat 0.5g); Cholesterol 55mg; Sodium 150mg; Total Carbohydrate 30g (Dietary Fiber 1g; Sugars 23g); Protein 3g **% Daily Value:** Vitamin A 8%; Vitamin C 0%; Calcium 4%; Iron 8% **Exchanges:** 1 Starch, 1 Other Carbohydrate, 3½ Fat **Carbohydrate Choices:** 2

chocolate mousse and meringue brownies

PAM FULTON
Woodinville, WA
Bake-Off® Contest 37, 1996

24 BROWNIES
PREP TIME: *30 minutes*
START TO FINISH: *3 hours 35 minutes*

BROWNIE CRUST
1 box (13.5 oz) Pillsbury® walnut
   brownie mix
¼ cup water
¼ cup vegetable oil
1 egg

MERINGUE
2 egg whites
⅛ teaspoon cream of tartar
½ cup sugar
½ cup chopped walnuts

MOUSSE
1 cup semisweet chocolate chips (6 oz)
3 tablespoons cold brewed coffee
   or espresso
½ teaspoon vanilla
1 cup whipping cream

1 Heat oven to 350°F. Grease bottom only of 13 × 9-inch pan with shortening or cooking spray. In large bowl, beat all crust ingredients 50 strokes with spoon. Spread in pan. Bake 15 minutes or until top is shiny. Remove from oven.

2 Reduce oven temperature to 250°F. In small bowl, beat egg whites and cream of tartar with electric mixer on medium speed about 1 minute or until soft peaks form. Gradually add sugar, beating on high speed until stiff, glossy peaks form. Spoon meringue evenly over warm partially baked brownie crust; spread carefully to within ¼ inch of sides. Do not allow meringue to touch sides of pan. Sprinkle walnuts over meringue. Bake 45 to 50 minutes or until meringue is dry and firm.

3 When brownies with meringue have baked 25 minutes, begin preparation of mousse. In 2-quart saucepan, heat chocolate chips and coffee over low heat, stirring occasionally, until chocolate is melted. Remove from heat. Add vanilla; stir until slightly thickened. Cool 20 minutes.

4 In large bowl, beat whipping cream on high speed until stiff peaks form. Fold cooled chocolate mixture into whipped cream. Spoon and spread over meringue. Refrigerate 2 hours. For brownies, cut into 6 rows by 4 rows. Store in refrigerator.

High Altitude (3500–6500 ft): Add 3 tablespoons all-purpose flour to dry brownie mix.

1 Brownie: Calories 190 (Calories from Fat 100); Total Fat 11g (Saturated Fat 4g; Trans Fat 0g); Cholesterol 20mg; Sodium 60mg; Total Carbohydrate 22g (Dietary Fiber 1g; Sugars 17g); Protein 2g **% Daily Value:** Vitamin A 2%; Vitamin C 0%; Calcium 2%; Iron 4% **Exchanges:** ½ Starch, 1 Other Carbohydrate, 2 Fat **Carbohydrate Choices:** 1½

amaretto coffee brownies

KEN HALVERSON

Big Lake, MN

Bake-Off® Contest 38, 1998

24 BROWNIES

PREP TIME: *25 minutes*

START TO FINISH: *2 hours 40 minutes*

12 oz cream cheese, softened

1 jar (7 oz) marshmallow creme (1½ cups)

2 tablespoons instant coffee granules or crystals

1 tablespoon amaretto or 1 teaspoon almond extract

1 box (19.5 oz) Pillsbury® fudge brownie mix

½ cup butter or margarine, softened

⅓ cup milk

2 eggs

¾ cup chopped walnuts

1 Heat oven to 350°F. Grease 13 × 9-inch pan with shortening or cooking spray. In large bowl, beat cream cheese, marshmallow creme, coffee granules and amaretto with electric mixer on medium speed until smooth; set aside.

2 In another large bowl, beat brownie mix and butter with electric mixer on low speed 45 to 60 seconds or until crumbly. Reserve 1 cup brownie mixture in small bowl for topping. Add milk and eggs to remaining brownie mixture; beat until smooth. Spread batter evenly in pan.

3 Spread cream cheese mixture evenly over brownie mixture. Stir walnuts into reserved 1 cup brownie mixture; sprinkle evenly over cream cheese mixture.

4 Bake 40 to 45 minutes or until edges are firm to the touch. Cool completely, about 1 hour 30 minutes. For brownies, cut into 6 rows by 4 rows. Store in refrigerator.

High Altitude (3500–6500 ft): Add ½ cup all-purpose flour to dry brownie mix. Bake 45 to 50 minutes.

1 Brownie: Calories 250 (Calories from Fat 120); Total Fat 14g (Saturated Fat 6g; Trans Fat 0g); Cholesterol 45mg; Sodium 150mg; Total Carbohydrate 27g (Dietary Fiber 1g; Sugars 20g); Protein 3g **% Daily Value:** Vitamin A 6%; Vitamin C 0%; Calcium 2%; Iron 8% **Exchanges:** 1 Starch, 1 Other Carbohydrate, 2½ Fat **Carbohydrate Choices:** 2

caramel-graham-fudge brownies

24 BROWNIES

PREP TIME: *30 minutes*

START TO FINISH: *2 hours 10 minutes*

GLORIA KATHLEEN GARDNER
Middleport, OH
Bake-Off® Contest 35, 1992

1 Heat oven to 350°F. In medium bowl, mix 1½ cups of the brownie mix, the graham cracker crumbs, sugar and butter. Press mixture in bottom of ungreased 13 × 9-inch pan.

2 In 2-quart saucepan, cook caramels and milk over medium heat, stirring constantly, until caramels are melted. Carefully spread melted caramel mixture over crust. Sprinkle with peanut butter chips, chocolate chips and ¾ cup of the pecans, reserving remaining ¼ cup pecans for topping.

3 In same medium bowl, beat remaining brownie mix, water, oil and egg 50 strokes with spoon. Carefully spoon batter evenly over pecans. Sprinkle with remaining ¼ cup pecans.

4 Bake 33 to 38 minutes or until center is set. Cool completely, about 1 hour. For brownies, cut into 6 rows by 4 rows.

High Altitude (3500–6500 ft): In step 3, add 2 tablespoons all-purpose flour to remaining dry brownie mix, then add water, oil and egg.

1 box (19.5 oz) Pillsbury® traditional fudge brownie mix

1½ cups graham cracker crumbs

½ cup sugar

½ cup butter or margarine, melted

1 bag (14 oz) caramels, unwrapped

⅓ cup evaporated milk (from 5-oz can)

¾ cup peanut butter chips

¾ cup semisweet chocolate chips

1 cup chopped pecans or walnuts

¼ cup water

¼ cup vegetable oil

1 egg

1 Brownie: Calories 350 (Calories from Fat 150); Total Fat 17g (Saturated Fat 5g; Trans Fat 0g); Cholesterol 20mg; Sodium 180mg; Total Carbohydrate 47g (Dietary Fiber 2g; Sugars 33g); Protein 4g **% Daily Value:** Vitamin A 4%; Vitamin C 0%; Calcium 4%; Iron 8% **Exchanges:** ½ Starch, 2½ Other Carbohydrate, 3½ Fat **Carbohydrate Choices:** 3

caramel-oatmeal brownies

CAROL ANN MARKFORD
Upper Darby, PA
Bake-Off® Contest 07, 1955

24 BROWNIES

PREP TIME: *25 minutes*
START TO FINISH: *1 hour 55 minutes*

BASE

⅓ cup Pillsbury BEST® all-purpose flour

½ cup packed brown sugar

1 cup quick-cooking oats

⅓ cup butter or margarine, melted

BROWNIES

2 oz unsweetened baking chocolate

½ cup butter or margarine

¾ cup granulated sugar

1 teaspoon vanilla

2 eggs

⅔ cup Pillsbury BEST® all-purpose flour

¼ teaspoon baking powder

¼ teaspoon salt

1 Heat oven to 350°F. In small bowl, stir together ⅓ cup flour, the brown sugar and oats until well blended. Stir in ⅓ cup melted butter until mixture is crumbly. Press firmly in ungreased 8-inch square pan. Bake 10 minutes.

2 In 1½-quart saucepan, melt chocolate and ½ cup butter over low heat, stirring frequently. Remove from heat; cool 5 minutes. Beat in granulated sugar and vanilla with wire whisk. Beat in eggs, one at a time. Stir in ⅔ cup flour, the baking powder and salt. Spread over partially baked base.

3 Bake 20 to 25 minutes or until center is set. Cool completely, about 1 hour. For brownies, cut into 6 rows by 4 rows.

High Altitude (3500–6500 ft): Bake 25 to 30 minutes.

1 Brownie: Calories 150 (Calories from Fat 70); Total Fat 8g (Saturated Fat 5g; Trans Fat 0g); Cholesterol 35mg; Sodium 85mg; Total Carbohydrate 18g (Dietary Fiber 0g; Sugars 11g); Protein 2g **% Daily Value:** Vitamin A 4%; Vitamin C 0%; Calcium 0%; Iron 6% **Exchanges:** 1 Starch, 1½ Fat **Carbohydrate Choices:** 1

peanut butter–honey brownies

16 BROWNIES

PREP TIME: *15 minutes*

START TO FINISH: *2 hours 20 minutes*

CHRISTIE BLANKFIELD
Grants, NM
Bake-Off® Contest 39, 2000

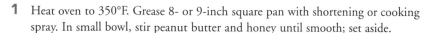

1 Heat oven to 350°F. Grease 8- or 9-inch square pan with shortening or cooking spray. In small bowl, stir peanut butter and honey until smooth; set aside.

2 In large bowl, beat brownie mix, ¼ cup butter, the water and egg 50 strokes with spoon. Spread half of batter in pan. Score batter into 16 squares (4 rows by 4 rows). Using ¼ cup of the peanut butter mixture, place scant measuring teaspoon mixture in center of each square. Carefully spread remaining brownie batter over top.

3 Bake 30 to 35 minutes or until edges pull away from sides of pan. Cool 45 minutes.

4 Spread remaining peanut butter mixture over brownies. In 1-quart saucepan, heat chocolate chips and 3 tablespoons butter over low heat, stirring constantly, until melted and smooth. Spoon and spread chocolate mixture over peanut butter mixture on brownies. Cool 45 minutes or refrigerate until set. For brownies, cut into 4 rows by 4 rows.

High Altitude (3500–6500 ft): Add ¼ cup all-purpose flour to dry brownie mix. Increase water to ¼ cup.

¾ cup creamy peanut butter

½ cup honey

1 box (15.5 oz) Pillsbury® chocolate chunk brownie mix

¼ cup butter or margarine, melted

3 tablespoons water

1 egg

¾ cup semisweet chocolate chips

3 tablespoons butter or margarine

1 Brownie: Calories 320 (Calories from Fat 150); Total Fat 17g (Saturated Fat 7g; Trans Fat 0g); Cholesterol 25mg; Sodium 180mg; Total Carbohydrate 39g (Dietary Fiber 2g; Sugars 30g); Protein 5g **% Daily Value:** Vitamin A 4%; Vitamin C 0%; Calcium 4%; Iron 8% **Exchanges:** ½ Starch, 2 Other Carbohydrate, ½ High-Fat Meat, 2½ Fat **Carbohydrate Choices:** 2½

peanut butter crunch brownies

CINDY EGERSDORFER
Cuyahoga Falls, OH
Bake-Off® Contest 42, 2006

24 BROWNIES

PREP TIME: *30 minutes*
START TO FINISH: *4 hours 10 minutes*

1 box (19.5 oz) Pillsbury® traditional fudge brownie mix

½ cup vegetable oil

¼ cup water

2 eggs

3 cups semisweet chocolate chips (18 oz)

1 bag (14 oz) caramels, unwrapped

¼ cup water

2 cups slightly broken pretzels (4½ oz)*

¼ cup butter or margarine, melted

1 cup powdered sugar

1 jar (18 oz) crunchy peanut butter

2 cups sweetened corn puff cereal with peanut butter and cocoa, slightly broken*

1 Heat oven to 350°F (325°F for dark pan). Grease 13 × 9-inch pan with shortening or cooking spray. In large bowl, make brownie mix as directed on box, using oil, water and eggs. Stir in 1 cup of the chocolate chips. Spread batter evenly in pan. Bake 28 to 30 minutes. Cool on cooling rack while making topping.

2 In medium microwavable bowl, microwave caramels and water uncovered on High 1 minute. Stir; continue to microwave in 15-second increments, stirring after each, until caramels are completely melted and mixture is smooth. Stir in broken pretzels until well coated. Spoon and spread carefully over cooled brownie layer.

3 In large bowl, mix melted butter and powdered sugar until smooth. Stir in peanut butter. Stir in broken cereal until well blended. Spread or pat over caramel layer.

4 In small microwavable bowl, microwave remaining 2 cups chocolate chips uncovered on High 1 minute. Stir; continue to microwave in 15-second increments, stirring after each, until chocolate is melted. Spread over cereal layer. Refrigerate 2 to 3 hours or until chocolate is set and caramel mixture is firm in center. Let stand at room temperature 10 minutes before cutting. For brownies, cut into 6 rows by 4 rows.

High Altitude (3500–6500 ft): Follow High Altitude brownie mix directions for 13 × 9-inch pan.

*To slightly break pretzels and cereal, place in separate resealable food-storage plastic bags; seal bags and break with rolling pin.

1 Brownie: Calories 530 (Calories from Fat 250); Total Fat 28g (Saturated Fat 9g; Trans Fat 0g); Cholesterol 25mg; Sodium 320mg; Total Carbohydrate 61g (Dietary Fiber 3g; Sugars 41g); Protein 9g **% Daily Value:** Vitamin A 2%; Vitamin C 0%; Calcium 6%; Iron 15% **Exchanges:** 2 Starch, 2 Other Carbohydrate, ½ High-Fat Meat, 4½ Fat **Carbohydrate Choices:** 4

praline brookies

JOANNA CRUMLEY
Hubbard, OR
Bake-Off® Contest 42, 2006

24 BROWNIES

PREP TIME: *20 minutes*
START TO FINISH: *1 hour 30 minutes*

1 box (19.5 oz) Pillsbury® traditional fudge brownie mix

½ cup vegetable oil

¼ cup water

2 eggs

¼ cup butter or margarine

¼ cup milk

½ cup granulated sugar

½ cup packed brown sugar

½ cup coarsely chopped pecans

½ teaspoon vanilla

1 roll (16.5 oz) Pillsbury® Create 'n Bake™ refrigerated chocolate chip cookies

1 Heat oven to 350°F (325°F for dark pan). Grease 13 × 9-inch pan with shortening or cooking spray. Make brownie mix as directed on box, using oil, water and eggs. Spread batter evenly in pan. Bake 25 minutes.

2 Meanwhile, in 2-quart saucepan, heat butter, milk, sugars, pecans and vanilla to boiling over medium heat, stirring constantly. Reduce heat to medium-low; simmer 3 minutes, stirring occasionally. Remove from heat; set aside until brownies are baked.

3 Immediately pour praline mixture evenly over partially baked brownies. Cut cookie dough crosswise into 4 equal pieces; cut each piece into 4 slices. Carefully place slices in 3 rows of 5 slices each, using last slice to fill in spaces. (Spaces between cookie dough pieces will spread during baking to cover top.)

4 Bake 23 to 28 minutes longer or until cookie topping is deep golden brown. Cool 2 hours. For brownies, cut into 6 rows by 4 rows.

High Altitude (3500–6500 ft): Follow High Altitude brownie mix directions for 13 × 9-inch pan. Bake 26 to 31 minutes.

1 Brownie: Calories 300 (Calories from Fat 130); Total Fat 14g (Saturated Fat 3.5g; Trans Fat 1g); Cholesterol 25mg; Sodium 140mg; Total Carbohydrate 40g (Dietary Fiber 1g; Sugars 30g); Protein 2g **% Daily Value:** Vitamin A 0%; Vitamin C 0%; Calcium 0%; Iron 8% **Exchanges:** ½ Starch, 2 Other Carbohydrate, 3 Fat **Carbohydrate Choices:** 2½

chewy butterscotch brownies

MRS. FLOYD DLOUHY

Granger, TX

Bake-Off® Contest 13, 1961

48 BROWNIES

PREP TIME: *40 minutes*

START TO FINISH: *1 hour 15 minutes*

BASE

¼ cup butter or margarine

1 cup coconut

½ cup packed brown sugar

½ cup chopped pecans

BROWNIES

1 cup packed brown sugar

½ cup butter or margarine

½ teaspoon vanilla

1 egg

1½ cups Pillsbury BEST®
  all-purpose flour

½ teaspoon baking soda

¼ teaspoon salt

½ cup miniature marshmallows

½ cup chopped pecans

1 cup miniature marshmallows,
  if desired

GLAZE

1 tablespoon butter or margarine

½ cup powdered sugar

¼ cup packed brown sugar

2 to 4 teaspoons milk

1 Heat oven to 350°F. Grease 13 × 9-inch pan with shortening or cooking spray. In 1-quart saucepan, melt ¼ cup butter over low heat. Stir in coconut, ½ cup brown sugar and ½ cup pecans. Spread evenly in bottom of pan.

2 In large bowl, beat 1 cup brown sugar and ½ cup butter with electric mixer on medium speed until blended. Beat in vanilla and egg. Stir in flour, baking soda and salt. Stir in ½ cup marshmallows and ½ cup pecans. Spoon dough over base; press with floured fingers over base.

3 Bake 20 to 23 minutes until light golden brown. Sprinkle with 1 cup marshmallows; bake 2 minutes longer. Cool completely, about 1 hour.

4 In 1-quart saucepan, melt 1 tablespoon butter. Stir in powdered sugar, ¼ cup brown sugar and enough milk until thin enough to drizzle. Drizzle glaze over brownies. Let stand 15 minutes until glaze is set. For brownies, cut into 8 rows by 6 rows.

High Altitude (3500–6500 ft): Decrease brown sugar in brownies to ¾ cup.

1 Brownie: Calories 110 (Calories from Fat 50); Total Fat 5g (Saturated Fat 2.5g; Trans Fat 0g); Cholesterol 15mg; Sodium 55mg; Total Carbohydrate 14g (Dietary Fiber 0g; Sugars 10g); Protein 0g **% Daily Value:** Vitamin A 2%; Vitamin C 0%; Calcium 0%; Iron 2% **Exchanges:** 1 Other Carbohydrate, 1 Fat **Carbohydrate Choices:** 1

white chocolate–almond brownies

24 BROWNIES

PREP TIME: *25 minutes*

START TO FINISH: *2 hours 35 minutes*

SALLY VOG
Springfield, OR
Bake-Off® Contest 33, 1988

1 Heat oven to 350°F. Grease 8-inch or 9-inch square pan with shortening or cooking spray. Reserve half of chopped white chocolate. In 1-quart saucepan, melt butter and remaining chopped white chocolate over low heat, stirring occasionally, until well blended.

2 In large bowl, beat sugar, salt and eggs with electric mixer on high speed about 4 minutes or until light in color. On low speed, beat in melted white chocolate mixture, vanilla and almond extract until well blended. Stir in flour and baking powder just until combined. Fold in reserved chopped white chocolate and the almonds. Pour into pan.

3 Bake 25 to 30 minutes or until center is set and top is light golden brown. Cool completely, about 1 hour.

4 In 1-quart saucepan, melt chocolate and shortening over low heat, stirring occasionally, until smooth; drizzle over brownies. Let stand until glaze is set, about 45 minutes. For brownies, cut into 6 rows by 4 rows.

High Altitude (3500–6500 ft): No change.

BROWNIES
10 oz white chocolate baking bars (from two 6-oz packages), chopped

¼ cup butter or margarine

½ cup sugar

⅛ teaspoon salt

2 eggs

1 teaspoon vanilla

¼ teaspoon almond extract

1 cup Pillsbury BEST® all-purpose flour

¼ teaspoon baking powder

2 tablespoons chopped almonds

GLAZE
1 oz semisweet baking chocolate, cut into pieces

1 teaspoon shortening

1 Brownie: Calories 140 (Calories from Fat 60); Total Fat 7g (Saturated Fat 4g; Trans Fat 0g); Cholesterol 25mg; Sodium 45mg; Total Carbohydrate 16g (Dietary Fiber 0g; Sugars 12g); Protein 2g **% Daily Value:** Vitamin A 0%; Vitamin C 0%; Calcium 4%; Iron 2% **Exchanges:** ½ Starch, ½ Other Carbohydrate, 1½ Fat **Carbohydrate Choices:** 1

candy bar brownies

ELIZABETH SEDENSKY
Cleveland, OH
Bake-Off® Contest 06, 1954

25 BROWNIES

PREP TIME: *15 minutes*
START TO FINISH: *1 hour 50 minutes*

2 bars (1.75 oz each) chocolate-covered coconut candy
½ cup shortening
1 cup sugar
1 teaspoon vanilla
2 eggs
1 cup Pillsbury BEST® all-purpose flour
½ teaspoon salt
½ cup chopped nuts

1 Heat oven to 350°F. Grease 9-inch square pan with shortening or cooking spray.

2 In 2-quart saucepan, melt candy bars and shortening over low heat about 3 minutes, stirring occasionally, until chocolate and shortening are melted. Stir in sugar and vanilla. Add eggs, one at a time, beating well with spoon after each addition. Stir in flour, salt and nuts. Spread in pan.

3 Bake 25 to 35 minutes or until top springs back when touched lightly in center. Cool about 1 hour. For brownies, cut into 5 rows by 5 rows.

High Altitude (3500–6500 ft): Decrease sugar to ¾ cup.

1 Brownie: Calories 130 (Calories from Fat 60); Total Fat 7g (Saturated Fat 2g; Trans Fat 0.5g); Cholesterol 15mg; Sodium 60mg; Total Carbohydrate 15g (Dietary Fiber 0g; Sugars 10g); Protein 2g **% Daily Value:** Vitamin A 0%; Vitamin C 0%; Calcium 0%; Iron 2% **Exchanges:** ½ Starch, ½ Other Carbohydrate, 1½ Fat **Carbohydrate Choices:** 1

Chocolate Buttersweets (page 129) ▶

praline butter nuggets

RUTH MAXWELL
Fort Smith, AR
Bake-Off® Contest 01, 1949

2 DOZEN COOKIES

PREP TIME: *1 hour 20 minutes*
START TO FINISH: *1 hour 20 minutes*

¼ cup granulated sugar
¼ cup pecan halves
1½ cups Pillsbury BEST®
  all-purpose flour
¼ cup packed brown sugar
¼ to ½ teaspoon salt
⅓ cup butter or margarine, softened
⅓ cup shortening
1 teaspoon vanilla
½ cup powdered sugar

1 Heat oven to 325°F. In 8-inch or 10-inch heavy skillet, melt granulated sugar over medium-low heat, without stirring, until golden brown. Stir in pecan halves until coated. Pour mixture onto sheet of foil. Cool 15 minutes or until hard. Finely chop pecan-sugar candy.

2 In small bowl, stir together flour, brown sugar and salt. In large bowl, beat butter, shortening and vanilla with electric mixer on medium speed until light and fluffy. Add flour mixture; beat until well combined. Stir in chopped pecan-sugar candy. (Dough will be crumbly.)

3 Shape dough into balls, using about 1 level measuring tablespoon dough for each; place on ungreased cookie sheets.

4 Bake 15 to 20 minutes or until set but not browned. Cool 5 minutes; remove from cookie sheets. Roll warm cookies in powdered sugar; place on cooling racks to cool.

High Altitude (3500–6500 ft): In step 1, stir granulated sugar and 2 teaspoons water in 8-inch or 10-inch heavy skillet until well mixed. With pastry brush dipped in water, brush any sugar down from sides of skillet. Heat over medium heat, without stirring, 10 to 12 minutes or until golden brown.

1 Cookie: Calories 110 (Calories from Fat 60); Total Fat 6g (Saturated Fat 2.5g; Trans Fat 0.5g); Cholesterol 5mg; Sodium 45mg; Total Carbohydrate 13g (Dietary Fiber 0g; Sugars 7g); Protein 0g **% Daily Value:** Vitamin A 0%; Vitamin C 0%; Calcium 0%; Iron 2% **Exchanges:** 1 Other Carbohydrate, 1 Fat **Carbohydrate Choices:** 1

sachertorte cookies

MRS. PHYLLIS WOLF
Salem, OR
Bake-Off® Contest 30, 1982

4 DOZEN COOKIES

PREP TIME: *1 hour 20 minutes*
START TO FINISH: *1 hour 35 minutes*

1 cup butter or margarine, softened

1 box (4-serving size) chocolate instant pudding and pie filling mix

1 egg

2 cups Pillsbury BEST® all-purpose flour

3 tablespoons sugar

⅔ cup apricot or cherry preserves

½ cup semisweet chocolate chips

3 tablespoons butter or margarine

1 Heat oven to 325°F. In large bowl, beat 1 cup butter and the pudding mix with electric mixer on medium speed until light and fluffy. Beat in egg. On low speed, gradually beat in flour.

2 Shape dough into 1-inch balls; roll in sugar. On ungreased cookie sheets, place balls 2 inches apart. With thumb, make indentation in center of each cookie.

3 Bake 15 to 18 minutes or until firm to the touch. Immediately remove from cookie sheets to cooling racks. Cool completely, about 15 minutes.

4 Fill each indentation with ½ teaspoon preserves. In 1-quart saucepan, melt chocolate chips and 3 tablespoons butter over low heat, stirring frequently, until smooth. Drizzle ½ teaspoon chocolate glaze over each cookie.

High Altitude (3500–6500 ft): Heat oven to 350°F. Bake 12 to 15 minutes.

1 Cookie: Calories 90 (Calories from Fat 50); Total Fat 5g (Saturated Fat 3.5g; Trans Fat 0g); Cholesterol 15mg; Sodium 65mg; Total Carbohydrate 11g (Dietary Fiber 0g; Sugars 5g); Protein 0g **% Daily Value:** Vitamin A 2%; Vitamin C 0%; Calcium 0%; Iron 2% **Exchanges:** 1 Other Carbohydrate, 1 Fat **Carbohydrate Choices:** 1

chocolate buttersweets

3 DOZEN COOKIES

PREP TIME: *1 hour 35 minutes*
START TO FINISH: *2 hours 15 minutes*

VANCE FLETCHER
Indianapolis, IN
Bake-Off® Contest 16, 1964

1 Heat oven to 350°F. In large bowl, beat ½ cup butter, ½ cup powdered sugar, the salt and 1 teaspoon vanilla with electric mixer on medium speed, scraping bowl occasionally, until blended. Gradually beat in 1 to 1¼ cups flour until soft dough forms.

2 Shape teaspoonfuls of dough into balls. On ungreased cookie sheets, place balls 2 inches apart. With finger, press hole in center of each.

3 Bake 12 to 15 minutes or until edges are lightly browned. Meanwhile, in small bowl, beat cream cheese, 1 cup powdered sugar, 2 tablespoons flour and 1 teaspoon vanilla on medium speed until well blended. Stir in walnuts and coconut.

4 Immediately remove cookies from cookie sheets to cooling racks. Spoon about ½ teaspoon filling into each cookie. Cool completely, about 30 minutes.

5 In 1-quart saucepan, heat chocolate chips, 2 tablespoons butter and the water over low heat, stirring occasionally, until chips are melted. Remove from heat. With spoon, beat in ½ cup powdered sugar until smooth. Frost cooled cookies.

High Altitude (3500–6500 ft): Bake 9 to 12 minutes.

COOKIES
½ cup butter or margarine, softened
½ cup powdered sugar
¼ teaspoon salt
1 teaspoon vanilla
1 to 1¼ cups Pillsbury BEST®
  all-purpose flour

FILLING
1 package (3 oz) cream
  cheese, softened
1 cup powdered sugar
2 tablespoons Pillsbury BEST®
  all-purpose flour
1 teaspoon vanilla
½ cup chopped walnuts
½ cup flaked coconut

FROSTING
½ cup semisweet chocolate chips
2 tablespoons butter or margarine
2 tablespoons water
½ cup powdered sugar

1 Cookie: Calories 110 (Calories from Fat 60); Total Fat 6g (Saturated Fat 3.5g; Trans Fat 0g); Cholesterol 10mg; Sodium 50mg; Total Carbohydrate 12g (Dietary Fiber 0g; Sugars 8g); Protein 0g **% Daily Value:** Vitamin A 2%; Vitamin C 0%; Calcium 0%; Iron 0% **Exchanges:** 1 Other Carbohydrate, 1 Fat **Carbohydrate Choices:** 1

almond party press cookies

MRS. JOHN H. LUIHN
Portland, OR
Bake-Off® Contest 03, 1951

ABOUT 9 DOZEN (2-INCH) COOKIES

PREP TIME: *1 hour 40 minutes*
START TO FINISH: *1 hour 40 minutes*

1 cup slivered almonds

2¼ cups Pillsbury BEST®
   all-purpose flour

¼ teaspoon salt

½ teaspoon ground cardamom

½ cup shortening

½ cup butter or margarine, softened

¾ cup sugar

1 egg

2 tablespoons milk

1 Heat oven to 350°F. In food processor or blender, place almonds. Cover; process until almonds are finely ground. Set aside.

2 In small bowl, stir together flour, salt and cardamom; set aside. In large bowl, beat shortening, butter and sugar with electric mixer on medium speed, scraping bowl occasionally, until light and fluffy. Beat in egg and milk. On low speed, beat in almonds and flour mixture until well blended.

3 Attach desired template to cookie press; place dough in cookie press. On ungreased cookie sheets, press dough into desired shapes.

4 Bake 7 to 10 minutes or until set and bottoms are golden brown. Immediately remove from cookie sheets.

High Altitude (3500–6500 ft): No change.

1 Cookie: Calories 40 (Calories from Fat 20); Total Fat 2.5g (Saturated Fat 1g; Trans Fat 0g); Cholesterol 0mg; Sodium 10mg; Total Carbohydrate 4g (Dietary Fiber 0g; Sugars 1g); Protein 0g **% Daily Value:** Vitamin A 0%; Vitamin C 0%; Calcium 0%; Iron 0% **Exchanges:** ½ Other Carbohydrate, ½ Fat **Carbohydrate Choices:** 0

spicy spritz cookies

ABOUT 8 DOZEN COOKIES

PREP TIME: *1 hour*

START TO FINISH: *1 hour*

S.M. CAMPBELL

Northbrook, IL

Bake-Off® Contest 11, 1959

1 Heat oven to 375°F. In medium bowl, stir together flour, ginger, cloves, cinnamon, baking soda and salt; set aside.

2 In large bowl, beat sugar and shortening with electric mixer on medium speed, scraping bowl occasionally, until light and fluffy. Beat in molasses, lemon extract and egg. On low speed, beat in flour mixture until well blended.

3 Attach template that has narrow slit with sawtooth edge to cookie press; place dough in cookie press. On ungreased large cookie sheets, press dough into 14-inch strips (on regular cookie sheets, press dough into 11-inch strips).

4 Bake 5 to 7 minutes or until edges are light golden. Cool 1 minute; cut into 2½-inch strips. Remove from cookie sheets.

High Altitude (3500–6500 ft): No change.

2 cups Pillsbury BEST® all-purpose flour

1 teaspoon ground ginger

1 teaspoon ground cloves

1 teaspoon ground cinnamon

½ teaspoon baking soda

½ teaspoon salt

¾ cup sugar

¾ cup shortening

3 tablespoons molasses

1 teaspoon lemon extract

1 egg

1 Cookie: Calories 35 (Calories from Fat 15); Total Fat 1.5g (Saturated Fat 0g; Trans Fat 0g); Cholesterol 0mg; Sodium 20mg; Total Carbohydrate 4g (Dietary Fiber 0g; Sugars 2g); Protein 0g **% Daily Value:** Vitamin A 0%; Vitamin C 0%; Calcium 0%; Iron 0% **Exchanges:** ½ Other Carbohydrate **Carbohydrate Choices:** 0

hawaiian cookie tarts

ELIZABETH ZEMELKO
Knox, IN
Bake-Off® Contest 34, 1990

36 COOKIE TARTS
PREP TIME: *35 minutes*
START TO FINISH: *2 hours 20 minutes*

COOKIES

1¾ cups Pillsbury BEST®
    all-purpose flour

½ cup powdered sugar

2 tablespoons cornstarch

1 cup butter or margarine, softened

1 teaspoon vanilla

FILLING

1 cup pineapple preserves*

½ cup granulated sugar

1 egg

1½ cups coconut

Additional powdered sugar (about
    2 tablespoons)

1 Heat oven to 350°F. In large bowl, stir together flour, ½ cup powdered sugar and the cornstarch. With spoon, beat in butter and vanilla until soft dough forms.

2 Shape dough into 1-inch balls. Place 1 ball in each of 36 ungreased mini muffin cups; press in bottom and up side of each cup. Spoon 1 teaspoon pineapple preserves into each dough-lined cup.

3 In small bowl, beat granulated sugar and egg with fork until well blended. Stir in coconut until well coated with egg mixture. Spoon 1 teaspoon coconut mixture over preserves in each cup.

4 Bake 23 to 33 minutes or until cookie crusts are very light golden brown. Cool in pans on cooling racks 20 minutes.

5 To release cookies from cups, hold muffin pan upside down at an angle over cooling rack. With handle of table knife, firmly tap bottom of each cup until cookie releases. Cool completely, about 15 minutes. Just before serving, sprinkle with additional powdered sugar.

High Altitude (3500–6500 ft): No change.

*In place of the pineapple preserves, ½ cup apricot preserves mixed with ½ cup drained crushed pineapple can be used.

1 Cookie Tart: Calories 130 (Calories from Fat 60); Total Fat 6g (Saturated Fat 4.5g; Trans Fat 0g); Cholesterol 20mg; Sodium 50mg; Total Carbohydrate 18g (Dietary Fiber 0g; Sugars 10g); Protein 0g **% Daily Value:** Vitamin A 4%; Vitamin C 0%; Calcium 0%; Iron 2% **Exchanges:** 1 Other Carbohydrate, 1½ Fat **Carbohydrate Choices:** 1

jamborees

MRS. RAYMOND KILDUFF
Harrisburg, PA
Bake-Off® Contest 08, 1956

5½ DOZEN SMALL COOKIES

PREP TIME: *1 hour 40 minutes*
START TO FINISH: *1 hour 40 minutes*

1 cup sugar
1¼ cups butter or margarine, softened
2 tablespoons vanilla
2 eggs
3 cups Pillsbury BEST® all-purpose flour
½ teaspoon salt
⅔ cup apricot preserves
⅓ cup finely chopped walnuts

1 Heat oven to 375°F. In large bowl, beat sugar and butter with electric mixer on medium speed, scraping bowl occasionally, until light and fluffy. Beat in vanilla and eggs. On low speed, beat in flour and salt until dough forms.

2 Attach star template to cookie press; place dough in cookie press.* On ungreased cookie sheets, press dough into 1½-inch diameter coils. Spoon ½ teaspoon preserves onto center of each coil. Sprinkle each with ¼ teaspoon walnuts.

3 Bake 8 to 12 minutes or until edges are light golden brown. Cool 1 minute; remove from cookie sheets.

High Altitude (3500–6500 ft): Bake 8 to 10 minutes.

*Or if desired, drop dough by rounded teaspoonfuls onto cookie sheets. Make indentation in center of each, using back of teaspoon dipped in cold water.

1 Small Cookie: Calories 80 (Calories from Fat 35); Total Fat 4g (Saturated Fat 2.5g; Trans Fat 0g); Cholesterol 15mg; Sodium 45mg; Total Carbohydrate 10g (Dietary Fiber 0g; Sugars 5g); Protein 0g **% Daily Value:** Vitamin A 2%; Vitamin C 0%; Calcium 0%; Iron 0% **Exchanges:** ½ Other Carbohydrate, 1 Fat **Carbohydrate Choices:** ½

sugar-crusted meltaways

3½ DOZEN COOKIES

PREP TIME: *1 hour 35 minutes*

START TO FINISH: *1 hour 35 minutes*

DOROTHY SHAFFER

Prosser, WA

Bake-Off® Contest 31, 1984

1 Heat oven to 325°F. In small bowl, mix orange peel and orange juice; set aside. In large bowl, beat ¼ cup sugar, the salt, butter, water and vanilla with electric mixer on medium speed, scraping bowl occasionally, until well blended. On low speed, beat in flour. Stir in chocolate chips and nuts.

2 Shape dough into 1-inch balls. Place 2 inches apart on ungreased cookie sheets.

3 Bake 15 to 20 minutes or until firm to the touch. Remove from cookie sheets to cooling racks. Cool completely, about 15 minutes.

4 Place fine strainer over another small bowl. Pour orange juice mixture through strainer to remove peel. Dip cooled cookies into orange juice; roll in additional sugar. Let stand until dry and sugar shell forms on each cookie.

High Altitude (3500–6500 ft): No change.

1 tablespoon grated orange peel

¼ cup orange juice

¼ cup sugar

⅛ teaspoon salt

¾ cup butter or margarine, softened

1 tablespoon water

1 teaspoon vanilla

1¾ cups Pillsbury BEST®
  all-purpose flour

1 cup semisweet chocolate chips (6 oz)

1 cup finely chopped nuts

Additional sugar (about ½ cup)

1 Cookie: Calories 100 (Calories from Fat 60); Total Fat 6g (Saturated Fat 3g; Trans Fat 0g); Cholesterol 10mg; Sodium 30mg; Total Carbohydrate 11g (Dietary Fiber 0g; Sugars 6g); Protein 1g **% Daily Value:** Vitamin A 2%; Vitamin C 0%; Calcium 0%; Iron 2% **Exchanges:** 1 Other Carbohydrate, 1 Fat **Carbohydrate Choices:** 1

crescent macadamia truffle cups

GLORIA PLEASANTS
Williamsburg, VA
Bake-Off® Contest 34, 1990

24 TRUFFLE CUPS
PREP TIME: *40 minutes*
START TO FINISH: *3 hours*

FILLING

4 oz sweet baking chocolate, cut into pieces

¼ cup unsalted butter, regular butter or margarine

¼ cup packed brown sugar

2 tablespoons Pillsbury BEST® all-purpose flour

2 tablespoons coffee-flavored liqueur or cold brewed coffee

1 egg

1 can (8 oz) Pillsbury® refrigerated crescent dinner rolls

24 whole macadamia nuts

TOPPING

3 oz white chocolate baking bar, cut into pieces

⅓ cup cream cheese spread (from 8-oz container)

½ cup whipping cream

2 tablespoons powdered sugar

1 teaspoon vanilla

1 Heat oven to 350°F. In 1-quart saucepan, melt sweet chocolate and ¼ cup butter over low heat, stirring constantly, until smooth. Remove from heat. Stir in brown sugar, flour, liqueur and egg; set aside.

2 Unroll dough into 2 long rectangles; firmly press perforations to seal. Cut each rectangle in half lengthwise. Cut each half crosswise into 6 (2-inch) squares. Press or roll out each square to 2¾-inch square. Place 1 square in each of 24 ungreased mini muffin cups; firmly press in bottom and up side, leaving corners of dough extended over edge of each cup.

3 Place 1 macadamia nut in each dough-lined cup. Spoon about 2 teaspoons filling mixture over nut in each cup.

4 Bake 12 to 15 minutes or until filling is set and corners of dough are golden brown. Cool 5 minutes. Remove from pan; place on cooling racks. Cool completely, about 30 minutes. Refrigerate until thoroughly chilled, about 1 hour.

5 In 1-quart saucepan, melt white baking bar and cream cheese over low heat, stirring constantly, until smooth. Cover with plastic wrap; refrigerate until thoroughly chilled, about 1 hour, stirring occasionally.

6 In small bowl, beat whipping cream, powdered sugar and vanilla with electric mixer on high speed just until soft peaks form. Add chilled white baking bar mixture; beat on low speed just until well blended. Pipe or spoon topping over top of chilled cups. Refrigerate until topping is set, about 30 minutes. Store truffle cups in refrigerator.

High Altitude (3500–6500 ft): No change.

1 Truffle Cup: Calories 160 (Calories from Fat 100); Total Fat 11g (Saturated Fat 5g; Trans Fat 0.5g); Cholesterol 25mg; Sodium 105mg; Total Carbohydrate 13g (Dietary Fiber 0g; Sugars 9g); Protein 2g **% Daily Value:** Vitamin A 4%; Vitamin C 0%; Calcium 2%; Iron 4% **Exchanges:** ½ Starch, ½ Other Carbohydrate, 2 Fat **Carbohydrate Choices:** 1

lemon kiss cookies

SANDI LAMBERTON
Solvang, CA
Bake-Off® Contest 33, 1988

6 DOZEN COOKIES

PREP TIME: *1 hour 15 minutes*
START TO FINISH: *2 hours 15 minutes*

¾ cup sugar

1½ cups butter or margarine, softened

1 tablespoon lemon extract

2¾ cups Pillsbury BEST®
   all-purpose flour

1½ cups finely chopped almonds

1 bag (13 oz) milk chocolate drops or
   pieces, unwrapped

Powdered sugar (about 1½ teaspoons)

½ cup semisweet chocolate chips

1 tablespoon shortening

1   In large bowl, beat sugar, butter and lemon extract with electric mixer on medium speed, scraping bowl occasionally, until light and fluffy. On low speed, beat in flour and almonds until well blended. Cover with plastic wrap; refrigerate at least 1 hour for easier handling.

2   Heat oven to 375°F. Shape 1 scant tablespoon dough around each milk chocolate candy, covering completely. Roll in hands to form ball. Place on ungreased cookie sheets.

3   Bake 8 to 12 minutes or until cookies are set and bottom edges are light golden brown. Cool 1 minute; remove from cookie sheets to cooling racks. Cool completely, about 15 minutes.

4   Lightly sprinkle cooled cookies with powdered sugar. In 1-quart saucepan, heat chocolate chips and shortening over low heat, stirring constantly, until melted and smooth. Drizzle over cooled cookie.

High Altitude (3500–6500 ft): Decrease butter to 1¼ cups.

1 Cookie: Calories 110 (Calories from Fat 70); Total Fat 7g (Saturated Fat 3.5g; Trans Fat 0g); Cholesterol 10mg; Sodium 30mg; Total Carbohydrate 10g (Dietary Fiber 0g; Sugars 6g); Protein 2g **% Daily Value:** Vitamin A 2%; Vitamin C 0%; Calcium 0%; Iron 2% **Exchanges:** ½ Starch, 1½ Fat **Carbohydrate Choices:** ½

chocolate tips

ABOUT 3 DOZEN SANDWICH COOKIES

PREP TIME: *1 hour 25 minutes*

START TO FINISH: *1 hour 40 minutes*

MRS. MARGUERITE DUGAN
Washington, D.C.
Bake-Off® Contest 04, 1952

1 Heat oven to 400°F. Grease cookie sheets with shortening or cooking spray. In medium bowl, beat butter and sugar with electric mixer on medium speed, scraping bowl occasionally, until light and fluffy. Beat in egg and vanilla. On low speed, beat in flour until well blended.

2 Attach template that has narrow slit with sawtooth edge to cookie press; place dough in cookie press. On large cookie sheets, press dough into 14-inch strips (on regular sheets, press dough into 11-inch strips).

3 Bake 6 to 8 minutes or until edges are light golden. Immediately cut into 2-inch pieces. Remove from cookie sheets to cooling racks. Cool completely, about 15 minutes.

4 Spread jelly over bottoms of half of the cookies (¼ teaspoon jelly each); top each with a cookie without jelly (place bottoms of cookies together). In 1-quart saucepan, heat chocolate chips and milk over low heat, stirring frequently, until chocolate is melted. Dip ends of sandwich cookies in melted chocolate, then in chocolate sprinkles.

High Altitude (3500–6500 ft): No change.

½ cup butter or margarine, softened

½ cup sugar

1 egg

1 teaspoon vanilla

1½ cups Pillsbury BEST®
   all-purpose flour

⅓ cup red raspberry jelly

½ cup semisweet chocolate chips

1 tablespoon plus 1½ teaspoons milk

¾ cup chocolate candy sprinkles or
   chopped nuts

1 Cookie: Calories 100 (Calories from Fat 40); Total Fat 4.5g (Saturated Fat 3g; Trans Fat 0g); Cholesterol 15mg; Sodium 20mg; Total Carbohydrate 13g (Dietary Fiber 0g; Sugars 8g); Protein 0g **% Daily Value:** Vitamin A 0%; Vitamin C 0%; Calcium 0%; Iron 2% **Exchanges:** 1 Other Carbohydrate, 1 Fat **Carbohydrate Choices:** 1

nutmeg cookie logs

MRS. ROBERT J. WOODS
South Charleston, WV
Bake-Off® Contest 08, 1956

5 DOZEN COOKIES

PREP TIME: *50 minutes*
START TO FINISH: *1 hour 35 minutes*

COOKIES

¾ cup granulated sugar

1 cup butter or margarine, softened

2 teaspoons vanilla

2 teaspoons rum extract

1 egg

3 cups Pillsbury BEST® all-purpose flour

1 teaspoon ground nutmeg

FROSTING

2 cups powdered sugar

3 tablespoons butter or margarine, softened

¾ teaspoon rum extract

¼ teaspoon vanilla

2 to 3 tablespoons half-and-half or milk

Additional ground nutmeg

1 In large bowl, beat granulated sugar, 1 cup butter, 2 teaspoons vanilla, 2 teaspoons rum extract and egg with electric mixer on medium speed until light and fluffy. With spoon, stir in flour and 1 teaspoon nutmeg. Cover with plastic wrap; refrigerate about 45 minutes for easier handling.

2 Heat oven to 350°F. Divide dough into 12 pieces. On floured surface, shape each piece of dough into long rope, ½ inch in diameter and about 15 inches long. Cut into 3-inch logs. On ungreased cookie sheets, place logs 1 inch apart.

3 Bake 12 to 15 minutes or until edges are light golden brown. Immediately remove from cookie sheets to cooling racks. Cool completely, about 20 minutes.

4 In small bowl, mix all frosting ingredients except nutmeg, adding enough half-and-half for desired spreading consistency. Spread on tops and sides of cookies. If desired, mark frosting with tines of fork to resemble bark. Sprinkle lightly with additional nutmeg. Let stand until frosting is set before storing.

High Altitude (3500–6500 ft): No change.

1 Cookie: Calories 80 (Calories from Fat 35); Total Fat 4g (Saturated Fat 2.5g; Trans Fat 0g); Cholesterol 15mg; Sodium 25mg; Total Carbohydrate 11g (Dietary Fiber 0g; Sugars 6g); Protein 0g **% Daily Value:** Vitamin A 2%; Vitamin C 0%; Calcium 0%; Iron 0% **Exchanges:** ½ Other Carbohydrate, 1 Fat **Carbohydrate Choices:** 1

split seconds

ROBERT E. FELLOWS
Silver Spring, MD
Bake-Off® Contest 06, 1954

4 DOZEN COOKIES

PREP TIME: *1 hour 15 minutes*
START TO FINISH: *1 hour 15 minutes*

⅔ cup sugar
¾ cup butter or margarine, softened
2 teaspoons vanilla
1 egg
2 cups Pillsbury BEST® all-purpose flour
½ teaspoon baking powder
½ cup red jelly or preserves

1 Heat oven to 350°F. In large bowl, beat sugar and butter with electric mixer on medium speed until light and fluffy. Beat in vanilla and egg until well blended. On low speed, beat in flour and baking powder until dough forms.

2 Divide dough into 4 equal parts. On lightly floured surface, shape each part into 12 × ¾-inch roll; place on ungreased cookie sheets. With handle of wooden spoon or finger, make indentation about ½ inch wide and ¼ inch deep lengthwise down center of each roll. Fill each with 2 tablespoons jelly.

3 Bake 15 to 20 minutes or until light golden brown. Cool slightly, 3 to 5 minutes. Cut each baked roll diagonally into 12 cookies; remove from cookie sheets.

High Altitude (3500–6500 ft): No change.

1 Cookie: Calories 70 (Calories from Fat 25); Total Fat 3g (Saturated Fat 2g; Trans Fat 0g); Cholesterol 10mg; Sodium 30mg; Total Carbohydrate 9g (Dietary Fiber 0g; Sugars 4g); Protein 0g **% Daily Value:** Vitamin A 0%; Vitamin C 0%; Calcium 0%; Iron 0% **Exchanges:** ½ Starch, ½ Fat **Carbohydrate Choices:** ½

frosted fruit jumbles

ABOUT 7 DOZEN COOKIES

PREP TIME: *1 hour 45 minutes*

START TO FINISH: *2 hours 45 minutes*

JEAN C. WEHLER
Hyattsville, MD
Bake-Off® Contest 15, 1963

1 Heat oven to 375°F. In large bowl, stir together flour, salt, baking soda, mace and nutmeg. Stir in candied fruit, raisins and walnuts; set aside.

2 In very large bowl, beat 1 cup butter, the brown sugar and granulated sugar with electric mixer on medium speed until light and fluffy. Beat in 1 teaspoon lemon extract, the vanilla and eggs. With spoon, stir in half of the flour-fruit mixture. Stir in sour cream. Stir in remaining flour-fruit mixture. Refrigerate at least 1 hour until chilled.

3 Shape dough by rounded teaspoonfuls into balls. On ungreased cookie sheets, place balls 2 inches apart. With bottom of glass dipped in granulated sugar, flatten to ¼-inch thickness.

4 Bake 9 to 12 minutes or until light golden brown. Remove from cookie sheets to cooling rack.

5 Meanwhile, in small bowl, mix 2 tablespoons butter, the powdered sugar and 1 teaspoon lemon extract. Stir in milk until smooth and spreadable. Frost warm cookies with glaze.

High Altitude (3500–6500 ft): Bake 8 to 11 minutes.

COOKIES

4 cups Pillsbury BEST® all-purpose flour

1 teaspoon salt

1 teaspoon baking soda

½ teaspoon ground mace

½ teaspoon ground nutmeg

2 cups mixed candied fruit

½ cup raisins

½ cup chopped walnuts

1 cup butter or margarine, softened

¾ cup packed brown sugar

½ cup granulated sugar

1 teaspoon lemon extract

1 teaspoon vanilla

2 eggs

⅓ cup sour cream

LEMON GLAZE

2 tablespoons butter or margarine, softened

2 cups powdered sugar

1 teaspoon lemon extract

2 to 3 tablespoons milk

1 Cookie: Calories 90 (Calories from Fat 30); Total Fat 3.5g (Saturated Fat 2g; Trans Fat 0g); Cholesterol 10mg; Sodium 70mg; Total Carbohydrate 15g (Dietary Fiber 0g; Sugars 9g); Protein 0g **% Daily Value:** Vitamin A 0%; Vitamin C 0%; Calcium 0%; Iron 2% **Exchanges:** 1 Other Carbohydrate, ½ Fat **Carbohydrate Choices:** 1

moonbeam cookies

JANICE OEFFLER
Danbury, WI
Bake-Off® Contest 39, 2000

3 DOZEN COOKIES

PREP TIME: *1 hour*
START TO FINISH: *1 hour*

1 roll (16.5 oz) Pillsbury® Create 'n Bake™ refrigerated sugar cookies

1 cup coconut

½ cup lemon curd (from 10-oz jar)

2 oz vanilla-flavored candy coating (almond bark), chopped, or ⅓ cup white vanilla baking chips

1 Heat oven to 350°F. In large bowl, break up cookie dough. Stir or knead in coconut. Shape dough into 1-inch balls. On ungreased cookie sheets, place balls 2 inches apart.

2 With thumb or handle of wooden spoon, make indentation in center of each cookie. Spoon about ½ teaspoon lemon curd into each indentation.

3 Bake 10 to 13 minutes or until edges are light golden brown. Remove from cookie sheets to cooling racks. Cool 5 minutes.

4 In small microwavable bowl, place candy coating. Microwave on Medium (50%) 2 minutes; stir well. Drizzle over cookies.

High Altitude (3500–6500 ft): No change.

1 Cookie: Calories 100 (Calories from Fat 40); Total Fat 4.5g (Saturated Fat 2g; Trans Fat 0.5g); Cholesterol 10mg; Sodium 50mg; Total Carbohydrate 15g (Dietary Fiber 0g; Sugars 11g); Protein 0g **% Daily Value:** Vitamin A 0%; Vitamin C 0%; Calcium 0%; Iron 0% **Exchanges:** 1 Other Carbohydrate, 1 Fat **Carbohydrate Choices:** 1

sugar–crusted almond pastries

KARLA KUNOFF
Bloomington, IN
Bake-Off® Contest 37, 1996

36 BARS

PREP TIME: *15 minutes*
START TO FINISH: *1 hour*

2 cans (8 oz each) Pillsbury®
  refrigerated crescent dinner rolls
½ cup butter (do not use margarine)
2 cups slivered almonds
1⅓ cups sugar

1 Heat oven to 375°F. Unroll both cans of dough into 2 large rectangles. Place in ungreased 15 × 10 × 1-inch pan; press over bottom to form crust, firmly pressing perforations to seal.

2 In 2-quart saucepan, melt butter over medium heat. Add almonds and sugar; cook 5 to 8 minutes, stirring frequently, until nuts just begin to brown. Spoon and spread mixture evenly over dough.

3 Bake 11 to 16 minutes or until crust is deep golden brown. Cool 30 minutes. For bars, cut into 6 rows by 6 rows. Serve warm or cool.

High Altitude (3500–6500 ft): In step 1, prebake crust 5 minutes. In step 3, bake 13 to 18 minutes.

1 Bar: Calories 140 (Calories from Fat 70); Total Fat 8g (Saturated Fat 2.5g; Trans Fat 1g); Cholesterol 5mg; Sodium 115mg; Total Carbohydrate 13g (Dietary Fiber 0g; Sugars 9g); Protein 2g **% Daily Value:** Vitamin A 0%; Vitamin C 0%; Calcium 0%; Iron 2% **Exchanges:** ½ Starch, ½ Other Carbohydrate, 1½ Fat **Carbohydrate Choices:** 1

raspberry–filled white chocolate bars

MARK BOCIANSKI
Wheaton, IL
Bake-Off® Contest 34, 1990

24 BARS
PREP TIME: *25 minutes*
START TO FINISH: *2 hours 20 minutes*

½ cup butter or margarine

1 bag (12 oz) white vanilla baking chips (2 cups) or 12 oz white chocolate baking bars, chopped

2 eggs

½ cup sugar

1 cup Pillsbury BEST® all-purpose flour

½ teaspoon salt

1 teaspoon amaretto or almond extract

½ cup raspberry spreadable fruit or jam

¼ cup sliced almonds, toasted*

1 Heat oven to 325°F. Grease 9-inch square pan or 8-inch square (1½-quart) glass baking dish with shortening or cooking spray; lightly flour. In 1-quart saucepan, melt butter over low heat. Remove from heat. Add 1 cup of the baking chips (or 6 oz chopped baking bar). LET STAND; DO NOT STIR.

2 Meanwhile, in large bowl, beat eggs with electric mixer on high speed until frothy. Gradually beat in sugar until lemon colored. On medium speed, beat in baking chip mixture. On low speed, beat in flour, salt and amaretto just until combined. Spread half of batter (about 1 cup) in pan. Set remaining batter aside.

3 Bake 15 to 20 minutes or until light golden brown.

4 Stir remaining 1 cup baking chips (or 6 oz chopped baking bar) into remaining half of batter; set aside. In 1-quart saucepan, melt spreadable fruit over low heat. Spread evenly over warm, partially baked crust. Gently spoon teaspoonfuls of remaining batter over spreadable fruit. (Some fruit may show through batter.) Sprinkle with almonds.

5 Bake 25 to 35 minutes longer or until toothpick inserted in center comes out clean. Cool completely, about 1 hour. For bars, cut into 6 rows by 4 rows.

High Altitude (3500–6500 ft): No change.

*To toast nuts, spread in ungreased shallow pan and bake at 350°F for 6 to 10 minutes, stirring occasionally, until light brown.

1 Bar: Calories 170 (Calories from Fat 80); Total Fat 9g (Saturated Fat 5g; Trans Fat 0g); Cholesterol 30mg; Sodium 110mg; Total Carbohydrate 21g (Dietary Fiber 0g; Sugars 16g); Protein 2g **% Daily Value:** Vitamin A 2%; Vitamin C 0%; Calcium 2%; Iron 2% **Exchanges:** 1½ Other Carbohydrate, 2 Fat **Carbohydrate Choices:** 1½

cherry truffle squares

48 BARS

PREP TIME: *15 minutes*

START TO FINISH: *1 hour 40 minutes*

CATHERINE STOVERN
Veteran, WY
Bake-Off® Contest 39, 2000

1 Heat oven to 350°F. Cut cookie dough in half crosswise. Cut each section in half lengthwise. With floured fingers, press dough in bottom of ungreased 13 × 9-inch pan to form base.

2 Bake 12 to 16 minutes or until light golden brown. Cool completely, about 45 minutes.

3 In medium microwavable bowl, microwave chocolate chips and butter uncovered on High 1 to 2 minutes, stirring every 30 seconds, until melted and smooth. Stir in cocoa, corn syrup and milk until well blended. Stir in powdered sugar until smooth. Press mixture over cooled crust. Top with cherries; gently press into filling.

4 In small microwavable bowl, microwave baking chips and shortening uncovered on High 30 seconds. Stir; continue microwaving, stirring every 10 seconds, until chips are melted and can be stirred smooth. Spoon and spread over filling. Refrigerate 20 minutes or until set. Cut into squares or diamond-shaped pieces. Garnish each with chocolate shavings.

High Altitude (3500–6500 ft): No change.

CRUST
1 roll (16.5 oz) Pillsbury® Create 'n Bake™ refrigerated sugar cookies

FILLING
⅓ cup semisweet chocolate chips

¼ cup butter

¼ cup unsweetened baking cocoa

3 tablespoons light corn syrup

1 tablespoon milk

2 cups powdered sugar

1 jar (10 oz) maraschino cherries (about 30 cherries), drained, chopped

TOPPING
1 cup white vanilla baking chips (6 oz)

2 tablespoons shortening

GARNISH, IF DESIRED
Chocolate shavings or curls

1 Bar: Calories 120 (Calories from Fat 45); Total Fat 5g (Saturated Fat 2.5g; Trans Fat 0.5g); Cholesterol 5mg; Sodium 45mg; Total Carbohydrate 17g (Dietary Fiber 0g; Sugars 13g); Protein 0g **% Daily Value:** Vitamin A 0%; Vitamin C 0%; Calcium 0%; Iron 0% **Exchanges:** ½ Starch, ½ Other Carbohydrate, 1 Fat **Carbohydrate Choices:** 1

caramel crisps

ESTHER VAN

La Porte, IN

Bake-Off® Contest 09, 1957

ABOUT 4 DOZEN (3-INCH) COOKIES

PREP TIME: *1 hour 10 minutes*

START TO FINISH: *1 hour 10 minutes*

1 cup packed brown sugar

½ cup butter or margarine, softened

⅓ cup shortening

½ teaspoon salt

2 tablespoons milk

1 teaspoon almond extract

1¾ cups Pillsbury BEST®
    all-purpose flour

¾ cup finely chopped almonds

Granulated sugar (about 1 tablespoon)

1 Heat oven to 350°F. In large bowl, beat brown sugar, butter, shortening, salt, milk and almond extract with electric mixer on medium speed until well blended, scraping bowl occasionally. On low speed, beat in flour and almonds.

2 On floured surface, roll half of dough at a time to ⅛-inch thickness. Cut into desired shapes with cookie cutters or pastry wheel. On ungreased cookie sheets, place shapes 2 inches apart. Sprinkle with granulated sugar.

3 Bake 8 to 10 minutes or until light golden brown. Cool 1 minute; remove from cookie sheets.

High Altitude (3500–6500 ft): No change.

1 Cookie: Calories 80 (Calories from Fat 40); Total Fat 4.5g (Saturated Fat 1.5g; Trans Fat 0g); Cholesterol 5mg; Sodium 40mg; Total Carbohydrate 9g (Dietary Fiber 0g; Sugars 5g); Protein 0g **% Daily Value:** Vitamin A 0%; Vitamin C 0%; Calcium 0%; Iron 2% **Exchanges:** ½ Other Carbohydrate, 1 Fat **Carbohydrate Choices:** ½

white chocolate–cinnamon triangles

32 BARS

PREP TIME: *10 minutes*

START TO FINISH: *1 hour 55 minutes*

ROBIN WILSON
Altamonte Springs, FL
Bake-Off® Contest 39, 2000

1 Heat oven to 350°F. In large bowl, break up cookie dough. Stir in remaining bar ingredients until well mixed. Press dough in bottom of ungreased 9-inch square pan.

2 Bake 23 to 27 minutes or until golden brown. Cool 30 minutes.

3 In small bowl, stir all glaze ingredients until smooth, adding enough milk for desired drizzling consistency. Drizzle over bars. Cool completely, about 45 minutes longer. For triangles, cut into 4 rows by 4 rows, then cut each bar in half diagonally.

High Altitude (3500°6500 ft): Bake 26 to 30 minutes.

BARS

1 roll (16.5 oz) Pillsbury® Create 'n Bake™ refrigerated sugar cookies

1 cup white vanilla baking chips (6 oz)

½ cup honey-roasted cashews or peanuts, chopped

½ cup toffee bits

1 teaspoon ground cinnamon

GLAZE

½ cup powdered sugar

¼ teaspoon ground cinnamon

2½ to 3 teaspoons milk

1 Bar: Calories 140 (Calories from Fat 60); Total Fat 7g (Saturated Fat 3g; Trans Fat 1g); Cholesterol 10mg; Sodium 75mg; Total Carbohydrate 18g (Dietary Fiber 0g; Sugars 14g); Protein 1g **% Daily Value:** Vitamin A 0%; Vitamin C 0%; Calcium 0%; Iron 0% **Exchanges:** ½ Starch, ½ Other Carbohydrate, 1½ Fat **Carbohydrate Choices:** 1

nutty chocolate chip biscotti

PAULA CONSOLINI
Williamstown, MA
Bake-Off® Contest 41, 2004

40 COOKIES
PREP TIME: *35 minutes*
START TO FINISH: *2 hours 40 minutes*

1 roll (16.5 oz) Pillsbury® Create 'n Bake™ refrigerated chocolate chip cookies

1½ teaspoons vanilla

½ teaspoon rum extract

1½ cups chopped almonds, hazelnuts (filberts) or pecans, lightly toasted*

1 cup semisweet chocolate chips

1. Heat oven to 350°F. Grease large cookie sheet with shortening or cooking spray; lightly flour. In large bowl, break up cookie dough. Sprinkle vanilla and rum extract over dough; mix well. Stir toasted almonds into dough.

2. Divide dough into 4 equal parts. Shape each part into 8 × 1-inch log. On cookie sheet, place logs 3 inches apart; flatten each log until about 1½ inches wide.

3. Bake 15 to 20 minutes or until golden brown. Cool 15 minutes. Reduce oven temperature to 200°F.

4. With serrated knife, carefully cut each log into 10 (¾-inch) slices. On same cookie sheet, place slices, cut side down.

5. Return to oven; bake at 200°F for 1 hour. Remove cookies from cookie sheet to cooling rack. Cool completely, about 20 minutes. Meanwhile, in small microwavable bowl, place chocolate chips. Microwave on High 1 minute. Stir; microwave 1 minute longer, stirring every 15 seconds.

6. Line cookie sheet with waxed paper. Dip ¼ of each cookie into melted chocolate; place on cookie sheet. Refrigerate about 10 minutes or until chocolate is set.

High Altitude (3500–6500 ft): Add ⅓ cup all-purpose flour to cookie dough in bowl.

*To toast nuts, spread in ungreased shallow pan and bake at 350°F for 6 to 10 minutes, stirring occasionally, until light brown.

1 Cookie: Calories 100 (Calories from Fat 50); Total Fat 6g (Saturated Fat 1.5g; Trans Fat 0g); Cholesterol 0mg; Sodium 35mg; Total Carbohydrate 11g (Dietary Fiber 0g; Sugars 7g); Protein 2g **% Daily Value:** Vitamin A 0%; Vitamin C 0%; Calcium 0%; Iron 2% **Exchanges:** 1 Other Carbohydrate, 1 Fat **Carbohydrate Choices:** 1

chocolate macaroon crescent bars

MISS JOY LYN BLANKSCHIEN
Clintonville, WI
Bake-Off® Contest 30, 1982

36 BARS

PREP TIME: *15 minutes*
START TO FINISH: *1 hour 20 minutes*

1 can (8 oz) Pillsbury® refrigerated crescent dinner rolls

2 cups coconut

1 can (14 oz) sweetened condensed milk (not evaporated)

⅛ to ¼ teaspoon almond extract

1 cup semisweet chocolate chips (6 oz)

2 tablespoons peanut butter

½ cup chopped almonds, if desired

1 Heat oven to 375°F. Spray 13 × 9-inch pan with cooking spray. Unroll dough and separate into 2 long rectangles; place lengthwise in pan. Press in bottom and ½ inch up sides to form crust; press edges and perforations to seal.

2 Sprinkle coconut evenly over crust. In medium bowl, mix milk and almond extract; drizzle over coconut.

3 Bake 16 to 20 minutes or until edges are golden brown and filling is set. Cool in pan on cooling rack 15 minutes.

4 In 1-quart saucepan, melt chocolate chips over low heat, stirring frequently. Stir in peanut butter. Spread chocolate mixture over bars; sprinkle with almonds. Refrigerate until chocolate is set, about 30 minutes. For bars, cut into 6 rows by 6 rows.

High Altitude (3500–6500 ft): No change.

1 Bar: Calories 110 (Calories from Fat 50); Total Fat 6g (Saturated Fat 3.5g; Trans Fat 0g); Cholesterol 0mg; Sodium 80mg; Total Carbohydrate 14g (Dietary Fiber 0g; Sugars 10g); Protein 2g **% Daily Value:** Vitamin A 0%; Vitamin C 0%; Calcium 4%; Iron 2% **Exchanges:** ½ Starch, ½ Other Carbohydrate, 1 Fat **Carbohydrate Choices:** 1

easy baklava bars

48 BARS

PREP TIME: *25 minutes*

START TO FINISH: *1 hour 45 minutes*

CAROL HAPPLEY

Jordan, MN

Bake-Off® Contest 33, 1988

1 Heat oven to 350°F. Grease 15 × 10 × 1-inch baking pan with shortening or cooking spray. Unroll dough into 2 long rectangles. Place in pan; press over bottom to form crust. Firmly press perforations to seal. Brush with 2 tablespoons melted butter. Bake 5 minutes. Remove from oven.

2 In large bowl, mix all filling ingredients. Spoon evenly over partially baked crust; gently press down. Bake 15 to 20 minutes longer or until golden brown.

3 In 1-quart saucepan, heat all glaze ingredients to boiling. Reduce heat; simmer 2 to 3 minutes, stirring constantly. Remove whole cloves. Drizzle glaze evenly over warm bars. Cool completely, about 1 hour. For bars, cut into 8 rows by 6 rows.

High Altitude (3500–6500 ft): Bake 20 to 25 minutes.

CRUST

1 can (8 oz) Pillsbury® refrigerated crescent dinner rolls

2 tablespoons butter or margarine, melted

FILLING

2 cups finely chopped walnuts

1 cup coconut

1 cup quick-cooking oats

2 tablespoons packed brown sugar

½ cup butter or margarine, melted

½ teaspoon ground cinnamon

⅛ teaspoon ground allspice

⅛ teaspoon ground cloves

GLAZE

½ cup granulated sugar

¼ cup water

¼ cup butter or margarine

2 tablespoons honey

1 tablespoon brandy, if desired

1 teaspoon lemon juice

¼ teaspoon ground cinnamon

3 whole cloves

1 Bar: Calories 110 (Calories from Fat 70); Total Fat 8g (Saturated Fat 3.5g; Trans Fat 0g); Cholesterol 10mg; Sodium 65mg; Total Carbohydrate 8g (Dietary Fiber 0g; Sugars 4g); Protein 1g **% Daily Value:** Vitamin A 2%; Vitamin C 0%; Calcium 0%; Iron 2% **Exchanges:** ½ Starch, 1½ Fat **Carbohydrate Choices:** ½

helpful nutrition and cooking information

Nutrition Guidelines

We provide nutrition information for each recipe that includes calories, fat, cholesterol, sodium, carbohydrate, fiber and protein. Individual food choices can be based on this information.

Recommended Intake for a Daily Diet of 2,000 Calories as Set by the Food and Drug Administration

Total Fat	Less than 65g
Saturated Fat	Less than 20g
Cholesterol	Less than 300mg
Sodium	Less than 2,400mg
Total Carbohydrate	300g
Dietary Fiber	25g

Criteria Used for Calculating Nutrition Information

- The first ingredient was used wherever a choice is given (such as ⅓ cup sour cream or plain yogurt).
- The first ingredient amount was used wherever a range is given (such as 3- to 3½–pound cut-up broiler-fryer chicken).
- The first serving number was used wherever a range is given (such as 4 to 6 servings).
- "If desired" ingredients and recipe variations were not included (such as sprinkle with brown sugar, if desired).
- Only the amount of a marinade or frying oil that is estimated to be absorbed by the food during preparation or cooking was calculated.

Ingredients Used in Recipe Testing and Nutrition Calculations

- Ingredients used for testing represent those that the majority of consumers use in their homes: large eggs, 2% milk, 80%-lean ground beef, canned ready-to-use chicken broth and vegetable oil spread containing not less than 65% fat.
- Fat-free, low-fat or low-sodium products were not used, unless otherwise indicated.
- Solid vegetable shortening (not butter, margarine, nonstick cooking sprays or vegetable oil spread as they can cause sticking problems) was used to grease pans, unless otherwise indicated.

Equipment Used in Recipe Testing

We use equipment for testing that the majority of consumers use in their homes. If a specific piece of equipment (such as a wire whisk) is necessary for recipe success, it is listed in the recipe.

- Cookware and bakeware without nonstick coatings were used, unless otherwise indicated.
- No dark-colored, black or insulated bakeware was used.
- When a pan is specified in a recipe, a metal pan was used; a baking dish or pie plate means ovenproof glass was used.
- An electric hand mixer was used for mixing only when mixer speeds are specified in the recipe directions. When a mixer speed is not given, a spoon or fork was used.

metric conversion guide

Volume

U.S. Units	Canadian Metric	Australian Metric
¼ teaspoon	1 mL	1 ml
½ teaspoon	2 mL	2 ml
1 teaspoon	5 mL	5 ml
1 tablespoon	15 mL	20 ml
¼ cup	50 mL	60 ml
⅓ cup	75 mL	80 ml
½ cup	125 mL	125 ml
⅔ cup	150 mL	170 ml
¾ cup	175 mL	190 ml
1 cup	250 mL	250 ml
1 quart	1 liter	1 liter
1½ quarts	1.5 liters	1.5 liters
2 quarts	2 liters	2 liters
2½ quarts	2.5 liters	2.5 liters
3 quarts	3 liters	3 liters
4 quarts	4 liters	4 liters

Weight

U.S. Units	Canadian Metric	Australian Metric
1 ounce	30 grams	30 grams
2 ounces	55 grams	60 grams
3 ounces	85 grams	90 grams
4 ounces (¼ pound)	115 grams	125 grams
8 ounces (½ pound)	225 grams	225 grams
16 ounces (1 pound)	455 grams	500 grams
1 pound	455 grams	½ kilogram

Measurements

Inches	Centimeters
1	2.5
2	5.0
3	7.5
4	10.0
5	12.5
6	15.0
7	17.5
8	20.5
9	23.0
10	25.5
11	28.0
12	30.5
13	33.0

Temperatures

Fahrenheit	Celsius
32°	0°
212°	100°
250°	120°
275°	140°
300°	150°
325°	160°
350°	180°
375°	190°
400°	200°
425°	220°
450°	230°
475°	240°
500°	260°

Note: The recipes in this cookbook have not been developed or tested using metric measures. When converting recipes to metric, some variations in quality may be noted.

index